EMIRATI WOMEN

JANE BRISTOL-RHYS

Emirati Women

Generations of Change

HURST & COMPANY, LONDON

First published in the United Kingdom in paperback in 2010 by
C. Hurst & Co. (Publishers) Ltd.,
41 Great Russell Street, London, WC1B 3PL
© Jane Bristol-Rhys, 2010
All rights reserved.
Printed in India by Imprint Digital

A Cataloguing-in-Publication data record for this book
is available from the British Library.

ISBN: 978-1-84904-098-3

www.hurstpub.co.uk

This is for Susan Koepsell because she always had confidence.

CONTENTS

Acknowledgments   ix

1. Generations of Change   1
2. Representations of Emiratis   25
3. Days of the Past   43
4. Our New Lives Behind Walls   57
5. Marriage, Education and Choices   83
6. Being Emirati Isn't Easy!   105
7. Traditions and the Future   125

References   135
Notes   139
Index   143

ACKNOWLEDGMENTS

This book is a result of hundreds of conversations, interviews and discussions over the course of eight and a half years. The debt I owe to the people who have shared their views, opinions and insights is enormous and I thank all of those who helped me to understand how Emirati women think about their lives. Many of my friends and acquaintances wish to remain anonymous and so I cannot name them here, but they know who they are and how grateful I am to them.

At Zayed University I have received the constant support of colleagues and friends for which I am very appreciative. David Chaudoir read an earlier version of this manuscript and was brave enough to point out inconsistencies and redundancies while standing in the same room with me. Thank you, David, for your keen eye and sharing your knowledge of the Emirates.

I would also like to thank Christopher Davidson for pushing me towards completion. Finally, thanks to Michael Allen who has always ensured that I had the time that was needed to get this done.

Abu Dhabi   30 January 2010

1

GENERATIONS OF CHANGE

I could see Maitha's grandmother as we drove into the family compound in Al Ain. She was sitting in her customary place on the low verandah that ran the length of the main house. I parked my car in front of an uncle's house, next to the separate *majlis* (receiving area) for visitors which was used by the family only when the heat was unbearable. It was early spring but in the United Arab Emirates that means warm temperatures and the afternoon was quite hot, but not nearly hot enough to persuade this grandmother that air conditioning was needed because that would mean moving inside, into the house or the *majlis*. She always preferred to be outside, supervising the coming and going of children, grandchildren, maids and gardeners, or tending to her farm and the corrals of animals at the rear of the compound.

'*Salaam alaikum.*' '*Keif halich?*' Conversation with Maitha's Grandma, whom we call Mama in Arabic, is always a bit of an ordeal for me and probably for her too, though we have gotten better over the years. I find it very difficult to understand her words that sounded muffled and seemed to fade behind her *burqah*. As long as she speaks quite loudly and I watch her eyes carefully we do seem to get on, much to the amusement of her daughters and granddaughters. After greeting one another we settled down on the edge of the verandah and waited for the coffee and dates to arrive. Maitha opened a package that had arrived from Canada, and when

1

her grandma asked '*Shoo hatha?*' she explained that the old missionary nurse, Doctura Latiefa, had sent her some pictures. '*Shoo aswar?*' '*Aswar min ayyam zaman huna fil Al Ain.*' Grandma immediately stretched out her hand to see the pictures of the old days in Al Ain. Soon Maitha's mother, Shamsah (Grandma's oldest child), joined us and then Grandpa wandered by to see what we were doing and got interested so sat down in a chair.

I had come simply to visit the family, but now the afternoon became very special and important to my understanding of how Emirati women remember the pre-oil past and, in the case of the young women born after the discovery of oil, how they thought about their history and what meaning it held for their lives now. Now I had three generations of the family sitting around me looking at pictures taken by a Canadian missionary forty-five years ago.

Grandma was little interested in the rolling dunes, soft sandy tracks through the desert or pictures of buildings under construction. She wanted to see pictures of people. Maitha flipped through the pile for her and pulled out all the people pictures. Grandma held each successive picture close to her face and studied the image intently. She then raised her head and gazed across the courtyard into the distance as if looking back in time. Then she would quickly look back at the picture she was holding, nod to herself in affirmation and then say the name out loud for the rest of us to hear. She was delicate with the prints, holding them reverentially, almost lovingly. I watched her closely. Her mouth was covered by the *burqah* of course, but her eyes, a very unusual grayish green, sparkled brightly as they darted to the next picture. The pictures, taken in the searing sunlight of the desert and in the deep shadows cast by palm frond walls and fences, with, I guessed, a 1960s vintage inexpensive camera, were sometimes so bright that you could feel the heat, and some, taken in the deep shade of the palm groves, were so dark that it was impossible to make out faces. Grandma tilted the photos back and forth in the light, straining to see the darkened faces.

I asked her if seeing these pictures brought back happy memories. 'They make me feel sad, really,' she said. Grandma looked down at the stack of photos in her lap. 'They have become strangers; we have all become strangers.' Her eyes no longer sparkled and she handed the photos to her daughter. 'Looking at those pictures just reminds me that our world has changed, nothing is the same, and no one cares what we have lost.' She stood up and announced that she had to check on things in the kitchen.

Shamsah and Maitha passed pictures back and forth. Shamsah paid close attention to those pictures that captured the poverty of the old days, the *'arish* (palm frond) houses that were little more than flimsy-looking huts, the ragged clothes worn by the people and the children's dirty faces and unkempt hair. She sighed, 'I remember those days. Look here, these women and children waiting at the hospital clinic. I sat there in the sand, in the shade of the *barasti* wall myself.' As she spoke I thought of her luxurious home in Abu Dhabi, her summers in London and cases of jewelry. 'Did that little girl ever imagine the life that she would live in the future?' Shamsah smiled but it was not a happy smile. 'No, she didn't.' I didn't press the issue. Shamsah abandoned Abu Dhabi city life at every opportunity and preferred to be in Al Ain where, she said, things were simpler and better.

Maitha, Shamsah's daughter, interrupted her examination of the pictures with 'Oh my God, look at this' and 'Wow, I had no idea.' She particularly liked a photo of several women carrying water pots on their heads. 'I never think that my grandmother did something like that,' she said. Then, quickly refocusing, she pointed out the bright colors of the long dresses worn by the women in the pictures. 'Look, polka dots, it's just like Umm Khammas on *Freej*! Like Jameelah, wow, vintage!' *Freej* is a popular Emirati television program whose animated 3–D stars are older Emirati women. In each episode the ladies are confronted by the new, modern, globalized Dubai that has grown up around their tiny little enclave of traditional-style stone houses that appears to be the sole surviving Emirati neighborhood, the *freej*. The program's opening sequence is a series of sweeping and swooping panoramic images of the new, highly urbanized Dubai whose tall buildings all appear to bend somewhat as if they are menacing the tiny little *freej*. A repeated theme in the program is that Emiratis are forgetting their traditions. The episode to which Maitha referred begins with the appearance of a young Emirati woman, Jameelah, who can barely speak Arabic and who seems to be permanently attached to her mobile phone. Jameelah takes one look at the four old ladies who are dressed in bright polka dot dresses and wearing wide *burqahs* that hide much of their faces and yells 'Oh wow, vintage!' The old ladies are appalled and quickly go to work on Jameelah in what might be called 'tradition boot camp.'

While it was very special to have the three generations of one family sitting together looking at pictures of the pre-oil days, the perspectives on the past and attitudes about the changes that had occurred which each of the women revealed were not entirely new to me. On that spring day I was just completing my fifth year of teaching at Zayed University in Abu Dhabi, and conversations, discussions, debates and arguments about the changing nature of Emirati society and social life had occupied much of my classes and research. In fact, I had used some of these same pictures in my classes to prompt discussions on life before oil and to illustrate features of Emirati material culture, such as plaiting palm leaves into mats and weaving goat hair for tent panels. For most of my students these pictures were a bit of a shock. They were accustomed to seeing the rather formally posed pictures of their rulers and other dignitaries gathered usually to open the first airport, the first high school and all the other firsts that happened so rapidly in the 1960s and early '70s. They had not seen pictures of families standing in the harsh sunlight, or women working and carrying water. The pictures they had seen were entirely male, and for most students they were remote and unconnected. The pre-oil past generally is so distant and dim that it has little meaning to younger Emiratis and oftentimes for their mothers as well. However, in reality the pre-oil days of hardship and poverty were less than fifty years ago and their grandmothers remember them in vivid detail.

In roughly two generations the rather isolated and impoverished communities of the southern Arabian Gulf, formerly known as the Trucial States, have been transformed into wealthy and globalized societies of the United Arab Emirates. Oil, which promised a better life, first meant payments for exploration and drilling and then complicated contractual agreements that parsed out the revenues first to foreign consortium stakeholders and then to the owners of the wells. The discovery of oil in commercial quantities in Abu Dhabi demanded immediate infrastructural development and facilities for the new industry. Oil not only fueled but also propelled the rapid urbanization and development that catapulted people into glittering new cities bustling with hundreds of thousands of foreigners who had come to work in the economic bonanza of nation-building (Abu Lughod 1983; Khalaf 2006). The change was so rapid that it is common to speak of pre-oil and post-oil time periods. Pre-oil carries with it connotations of poverty, isolation, dependency and a degree of backwardness; there is too the implicit assumption of equilibrium. The pre-oil UAE is characterized by timelessness and stagnation. Post-oil is another world entirely, one that is characterized by expansion, improvement, wealth and change. The speed and the scope of development that occurred in the post-oil period have been so dramatic that they have affected every aspect of Emirati culture and society, creating a rupture in the local life pattern (Khalaf 2002:18). This rupture is made manifest when Emiratis narrate their social history because, for many, only post-oil life is worth remembering or talking about (Bristol-Rhys 2009).

It is almost impossible to avoid superlatives when writing about the changes that have occurred in this small country. Rapid, breathtaking, amazing, mindboggling, stunning and unbelievable have all been used to describe the wide-ranging construction projects and infrastructural development that built the UAE so quickly. That same sense of urgency exists today, as the major cities of Abu Dhabi and Dubai now seem to be competing over scale, grandeur and international recognition (Davidson 2007; 2008). The international media report frequently on the UAE with articles on the number of construction cranes in the country, more than a quarter of the world's inventory; the working and living conditions of the laborers, slowly improving; the amount of money invested in all these projects, in the billions of dollars; and just how high the tallest building will be, finally. Underneath all the media hyperbole and excessive superlatives is a population of less than a million Emiratis who are living lives that their great-grandparents would not have been able to imagine. This book explores some of the ways in which Emirati women have adapted to the swift development, urbanization and globalization that have brought university education, medical care, enormous villas, luxurious cars, maids, drivers, designer labels and summer homes in Europe in less than four decades. It also explores how women perceive the changes in their lives and what they believe has been lost along the way. For the last eight years I have lived in Abu Dhabi and taught female Emirati university students. As my friendship with former students and their female relatives has grown, I have been included in family events, along with grandmothers, aunts and cousins, planning engagements and weddings, sitting together while we wait for the birth of a new family member, and traveling abroad with families in the summer. We have discussed the differences in clothing, language, behavior and old lives, new lives and future lives in a country that though once was mired in timelessness seems now never to rest.

That restlessness is apparent in many ways in Emirati cities. To most observers, Emiratis seem never to be satisfied with the present and are constantly building new—hotels, resorts, houses, office blocks, planned cities, themed villages, cultural districts, and man-made islands; and buying new—cars, clothes, furniture, decorations, appliances, jewels and property in other countries. Cranes are visible all over the island city of Abu Dhabi, and city streets and roads are constantly under reconstruction and expansion. The city's future, unveiled in the Abu Dhabi 2030 strategic plan, indicates that construction will intensify over the next decade with US$ 163 million to be invested in the infrastructure, tourism, mass transit and the development of new residential areas (Willington 2007). These ambitious plans for growth and the post-modern design of the buildings, bridges and complexes—commercial, cultural and residential—raise eyebrows and questions. Who is going to live and work in these new developments? The number of foreigners in the country has long been an issue of concern for Emiratis, and that has intensified recently with new influxes of construction workers and the growing realization that what is being built is designed for 'Western' lifestyles, not Emirati. Few complaints are aired publically; Emiratis do not typically vent publicly in newspapers, though they may in the culturally sanctioned outspokenness of a *majlis* at a ruler's residence, the institutionalized gathering of (mostly) men in which they may address a sheikh directly. The many with whom I have discussed the 'new Abu Dhabi' shrug with resignation. 'What can we do? Decisions are made without discussion and without regard to what we think.' 'To complain is both a waste of energy and might well be just asking for trouble.' In fact, the country's media law forbids criticizing the government, reporting on stories that might be damaging to the economy or disparaging to all the members of the ruling families of each of the seven emirates and, by extension, their decisions (Watch 2009). Since it is the ruling families that own the land, public criticism about real estate development is essentially stifled. It is difficult to gauge what the Emirati level of criticism is for many reasons. First and probably foremost is the fact that the UAE is essentially a welfare state and the citizens are well-provided for throughout their lives. Second, access to jobs, resources, promotions, placements for children, land for houses and even invitations to weddings are all linked to one's social reputation and standing—if you are out of favor, you are out of luck. Having said that, I must also note that some of the most vehement criticism that I have heard comes from Emiratis who are very much in favor and whose lifestyles reflect their close connection to the ruling family. However, there is a generalized atmosphere of suspicion about being heard to be critical—in fact, even to be overheard discussing some topics. Mobile phones are turned off and put in purses and briefcases before some issues are discussed, and I have several friends who speak freely only when we are out of the country.

Thirdly, Emiratis are—here willfully ignoring the anthropological caveat not to generalize about a people—very sensitive to criticism. 'We were criticized for being poor, illiterate Bedouin and now we are criticized for being rich! Nothing we do will ever be 'right' and 'accepted' because the West will always claim that we are copying them; and the rest of the Arab world thinks of us as rich upstarts who should spend all our money solving their problems.' There is a great amount of truth in both those statements, and the 'dissing' of Emiratis by foreigners is common and frequently brutal.

While Emiratis may joke ironically that shopping is the national sport, they do so with chagrin because they are very conscious that this draws jealousy, ire and criticism from foreigners. The women of the wealthier families do spend much of their time shopping with what appears to be little regard for what they are spending. The level of very conspicuous consumption is often the first characteristic noticed about Emiratis, and they are described rather disparagingly as 'filthy rich with no taste' and accused of nouveau riche spending because suddenly 'they can.' Emiratis have in fact been stereotyped quite harshly as wealthy, lazy and arrogant, though not as badly as some of their Gulf neighbors like the Kuwaitis who, it seems, have quite a bad reputation wherever they go.[1] Emiratis have also been labeled stand-offish to foreigners, said to be formally polite but yet not quite friendly enough for some. It is in their own country that Emiratis seem to be most vilified, and this by the huge expatriate populations who live and work there. Emirati concerns about culture, identity and being a shrinking minority population within their own country are often dismissed as irrelevant because the lifestyle that most enjoy is enviable. The construction of extravagant buildings like the gold encrusted Emirates Palace Hotel and the Frank Gehry designed Guggenheim on Saadiyat Island, teenagers driving Hummers, social benefits that include medical care, higher education, comfortable pensions, as well as spacious villas that are kept in order by armies of maids, gardeners and cooks, make quite an impression, but not one of a people overcome with worry. When traveling abroad, as many families do in the unbelievably hot summer months, the word 'Emirati' is synonymous with shopping excess. So many Emirati families go to London during the summer that the joke is you'd be better off learning Emirati Arabic in Harrods' Ladurée tea room than in the UAE. In fact, the Emiratis getting in and out of the cars lined up at Harrods' entry door number 3 (the only entry to use, I am told) are inevitably the UAE's most powerful and wealthy. Etihad, Abu Dhabi's airline, adds extra cargo flights to accommodate the summer shopping that is shipped home on the family's return. Since I am always the beneficiary of a small part of this shopping largesse I can hardly complain.

It is the excess, sadly, that is so visible—whether in Abu Dhabi or London. I have met many expatriates, 'expats' as they're called, who have lived in Abu Dhabi for several years and yet never once have had a conversation with an Emirati. They see Emiratis in the malls, shopping, chatting in coffee shops, going into cinemas and walking around. There is no contact or communication. Many, indeed most, expats work in companies that have been staffed exclusively if not predominantly by foreign employees, and so they are often separated at work too. Unfortunately this separation has engendered stereotypes, urban myths and fears that are repeated within the various expat societies. The most commonly heard is that 'they're all lazy' and this is usually followed by 'they never had to work a day in their life so they aren't capable.' The urban myths are stories such as 'my friend said he saw an Emirati shoot the tires out on his Range Rover because it ran out of petrol' and 'their maids are just sex slaves, you know, it's terrifying.' Expats worry too about the presumed negative consequences of an unavoidable interaction with an Emirati. 'God, never have a car accident with one, you would be at fault no matter what really happened!' 'Be careful what you say at bars, there's always someone there listening to conversations, but they're hard to spot when they're not wearing national dress.'

There are several factors that encourage these stereotypes. First, it is entirely possible to live and work in the UAE for an extended period of time without interacting with Emiratis. In fact, most visitors will only speak to the young Emiratis sitting in the passport control booths at one of the airports. From that point on baggage porters, airline representatives, taxi drivers, hotel employees, restaurant staff, shop attendants and even many of the police are non-Emiratis. Not only are Emiratis outnumbered by foreigners, they also generally do not work in service sectors or at what they consider to be menial jobs. There are exceptions to this, for example the customer assistance people at Etisalat, the national telecommunications company, the post office, electric and water utility and other official offices such as vehicle registration. Emiratis generally work in the ministries of the government, in the public sector, as it is called. The public sector is now under some rather intense scrutiny for being over-staffed and inefficient, and the government is encouraging Emiratis to seek employment in the private sector. Companies in the private sector are more than a little resistant because of the higher wages and benefits packages that Emiratis command by comparison to foreign workers.

Emiratis are very noticeable on the streets of the cities. Like their neighbors in the other Gulf States, Emiratis wear what is often referred to as 'national dress.' Most commonly this is a white full-length *kandoura* for men and black *'abayah* over-garment for women. In the cooler months men wear colored *kandoura* made of heavier cloth than the light summer versions. Each country has adopted particular distinctions to national dress that clearly identify a Saudi from a Qatari or an Emirati. Saudi *kandoura* characteristically sport a Nehru-style collar, while the Qatari have a pointed shirt collar and the Emirati style has no collar at all. The *'abayah*, a loose-fitting, full-length black over-garment worn by women, has been adopted elsewhere by Muslim women and so it is becoming less a clear signal of Gulf citizenship. However, in Abu Dhabi the *'abayah* remains a fairly clear indication of nationality: either Emirati or another Gulf country. It is not very common to see a non-Emirati woman wearing an *'abayah*, and the motivation for doing so is somewhat suspect as a tall blonde woman leaving a hotel in the wee hours of the morning is easily branded no matter what she is wearing. An Emirati woman can instantly recognize a fraudulent 'national' on the basis of the cut of the *'abayah*, how it is worn, and the wrap of the *shaylah*, the headscarf, and a myriad of other clothing clues that are immediately apparent to them and still remain rather obscure to me. In cases where the woman might have donned the *'abayah* out of piety and perhaps respect for her Emirati hosts, my friends express mild amusement with the fact that someone would choose to wear the national dress of another country when they may have one of their own. In the other sort of cases, those in which the *'abayah* is worn with little piety and less respect, the reaction is venomous. One Emirati friend challenged a Maghrebi, a North African woman, who was wearing an *'abayah* one afternoon in a trendy shop in one of the malls in Abu Dhabi. My friend was civil, but the implication that this woman wasn't fooling anybody was clear and if she was fishing for Emirati men she would have to do better than wearing an 'abayah.

On the roads Emirati are easily recognizable as well. The equivalent of national dress for cars is to have the windows tinted so dark that it is impossible to see inside the vehicle. Only Emiratis are permitted to have windows tinted to that extent and the car must be registered to a married Emirati man. The rationale for this is that the women of the family should not be seen by strangers as they ride in the car. Sleek luxury cars and behemoth SUVs with darkened windows are as clear a sign of citizenship as is national dress. The cars deposit women and children at malls and shops. If they are using a driver, he finds a nearby place to park and wait for the mobile phone call that will summon him back to pick them up. Valet parking is available at most of Abu Dhabi's malls and even some hospitals, so even without a driver there is no need to park and walk. One friend's daughter was struck speechless at the prospect of walking from our spot in the parking lot into Marina Mall, one of the shopping malls in Abu Dhabi. She recovered nicely and walked the short distance while laughing about being so lazy. Later I heard her confiding to a friend on the phone that she had been shopping with me without the driver and that we had walked! It is amusing to be such a catalyst of change.

Although Emiratis may be identifiable and noticeable, rumors of their imminent extinction remain prevalent among the naive. One such tale is that when a visiting journalist asked a British woman in Dubai where he could find Emiratis to speak to for his story, she told him that 'they were all gone, well almost, and the few that are left are up in the mountains somewhere' (Krieger 2007). I am asked frequently by newcomers and visitors how I like working with Emiratis, and the tone of their questions seems to imply that I am working on a reservation somewhere for which I must have had special training. Many of these same people express surprise that there are enough Emiratis to fill a university. They seem quite stunned when I tell them there are three national institutions and that one, Higher Colleges of Technology, has sixteen campuses.

In addition to being outnumbered and apparently hard to find, Emiratis tend to socialize within family groups. There are exceptions to this of course: men host guests for dinners at restaurants, open their *majlis* (the formal entertaining area) to friends and associates and spend time chatting with friends in coffee shops. These are quite exclusively male gatherings and rarely include non-Emirati men unless it is a business dinner or a special *iftar* evening meal during Ramadan, during which all colleagues, business partners and acquaintances may well be invited. At the fundamental level of relaxing, visiting and sharing a meal, Emiratis usually do not go outside of their extended family group. This is especially true for women. School, college and university study are changing this as women maintain friendships long after graduation, but that change has been slow. Wedding celebrations, which I will discuss in depth later, are important events, and there Emirati women may socialize with women to whom they are not related in the public venue of a hotel or wedding tent. Endurance horse racing is quite popular among younger, affluent Emirati women, and the horse races attract competitors from all over the country and so are providing new opportunities to socialize with women outside of the family.

In all significant ways Emirati society is a tightly knit and rather closed society that revolves around the extended family. This can be quite enormous because it is not uncommon to have four or five uncles and as many aunts on both sides of the family. In fact, in the case of first-cousin marriage, which is their ideal arrangement, all the siblings of both parents are considered as the immediate family. The preferred residential pattern is patrilocal, and the ideal is for the brothers and their wives and children to share a large family compound whose center is the father if he is still alive. Polygamy, or more accurately polygynny, is legal and practiced. There is a dearth of information on marriage patterns in the pre-oil days, except for anecdotal stories about rulers marrying frequently for political and social ends. It appears that polygamous marriages occurred primarily among the wealthier merchant families and the rulers (Heard-Bey 1982:148). With post-oil affluence, multiple wives have become more common than they were, but without accessible statistics this is hard to measure.[2] In the case of multiple wives, if the first wife is Emirati, she and her children will live in the patrilocal compound. Later, additional wives, no matter what nationality, will have separate houses or apartments. There are no hard and fast rules for interaction between the multiple wives and their children, but generally wives avoid interaction if they can help it, as do their children. Newly married couples may live in the family home of the groom for some time if a suitable house has not yet been built or if one or other of the couple is finishing university or perhaps considering taking a job in another Emirate that would require commuting during the week.

The men of the family are usually absent from the home during the evenings. Besides socializing, a significant portion of Emirati business is conducted during the hours after sunset, especially in the hot months. There are too the important open *majlises* that are held by the rulers in which events are discussed, petitions made and assistance sought. The average evening for an Emirati family usually includes visits from aunts and cousins, the younger ones sprawled out on the floor of the living room or kitchen, working on homework or watching TV. Meals are often cooked in one central kitchen in the compound and then delivered by maids to the various residences, but more commonly the women of the family will eat together in one house along with the children. If the women of the family are not anticipating visits from maternal aunts and cousins they will most likely set out to visit or shop. Visiting one's relatives is mandatory. If you have not gone to visit someone, you will be receiving guests at your home. Most visiting is arranged by telephone two or three days in advance, except of course among the immediate family. Visiting takes place in the early evening, beginning about 6.30 or 7.00, and normally does not include a full meal. Guests are welcomed with the slightly bitter coffee, *gahwa*, which is always served with dates. Juices, teas and more coffee will be served along with sweets and chocolates throughout the visit. Great care is given to dress, make-up and jewelry for visits. Unmarried daughters always accompany their mothers on visits and the daughters of the house must welcome them into the home. Prominent wealthy families and members of the ruling family have frequent visits by non-kin women and the wives of their husbands' foreign business associates, but these normally occur on special holidays or for special reasons like welcoming the women back

13

from *umra* or *hajj* pilgrimages, the birth of a baby, recovering from illness or an impending marriage.

So, for the many expats who live in the UAE it is a rare occasion that takes them into an Emirati home. For a man a visit means entry only into the formal entertaining room, the *majlis*; this may be a separate structure or a room in the house that is adjacent to the front entry and is situated so that it provides no views into the interior rooms where the women of the family might be sitting. A woman's experience would be quite different and she would be welcomed into the interior of the house, to the women's sitting area that is also the family area. First visits are often tensely formal with the welcoming coffee and dates, then perhaps *chai haleeb*, which is tea with milk and sugar, and sweets of some sort. Conversations usually stick to children, shopping, clothes and subjects that are safe and familiar to both sides. Older Emirati women often do not speak English, or speak it rather haltingly, and this too can put limits on what is discussed with foreign visitors. Many expatriate women complain about their 'hideous' evenings during Ramadan when they 'had to go visit' and were forced to sit for hours sipping tea and eating sweets while not knowing what to say next. Similarly, one or two wedding celebrations are usually the limit for expatriates who chafe against the large crowds, the seating arrangements, the unfamiliar food (often young camel is served), and, most commonly, the fact that the celebrations go on 'forever'.

I have slowly developed a taste for young camel but rarely do I manage to stay until the wedding celebration draws to a close at three in the morning. I have attended some fifty weddings and now go in the company of a group of Emirati friends who are very selective about which weddings we should go to. They have taken to dressing me in very traditional-style clothes for the weddings we do attend—a fact that draws a great amount of attention from the other guests and lots of compliments—not to me, but to my fashion consultants. At a recent wedding one woman asked why I would agree to wear a traditional-style dress, and before I could answer my friend interjected 'because she studies our traditions and likes them more than we seem to do!'

14

My interest in Emirati society, past and present, has, in many ways, been the means by which I have been accepted by Emirati families. When I first walked into a classroom my knowledge of the country and the people was rudimentary at best, and as my knowledge expanded so did the questions that I asked my students. In the beginning the students often looked surprised at my questions and would offer a simple, short explanation. As I persisted and persevered, they would often admit that they didn't know and would have to ask their mother or grandmother. There were two years of questions and answers going back and forth between classes and homes before I was invited to meet the people who were answering my questions. Why, I asked, had it taken so long to be taken to meet your mothers and grandmothers? 'Because they were concerned, almost embarrassed, to meet you; after all, you're a professor and my grandmother cannot read.' And why now the change, I asked? 'You keep asking, you don't give up and grandmother wants to make sure you learn it right!'

Learning it right meant more than beginning to understand and appreciate Emirati culture; it also meant delving into the transnational and multicultural society in which Emiratis live. It is safe to say that an Emirati sees more foreigners on any given day than they do other Emiratis. The major cities of the country—Abu Dhabi, Dubai, Sharjah and Ras al Khaimah—owe their existence to the labor of foreigners. So ubiquitous are foreigners—myself included—that it is hard to imagine a time when there were relatively few.[3] The grandmothers who have talked to me do remember and they are saddened by the changes, fueled by oil wealth and foreigners, that have reshaped their lives. Their daughters were the first generation of girls to go to school and, according to their mothers, to become spoiled and lazy. My students, in their late teens and early twenties, have known only houses cleaned by maids, children minded by nurses and nannies, meals presented by cooks and drivers to take them to school.

Foreigners are often lumped into one large catch-all phrase as in 'we are surrounded by foreigners.' In reality there are significant distinctions that divide the foreign population of the country. Laborers are always male and most usually South Asian. These men are contracted by labor-brokering companies in their home countries and then re-contracted to construction and industrial companies in the UAE. Workers are one notch up from laborers and may be either male or female. Maids, drivers, gardeners, taxi drivers, shop attendants and delivery personnel are all considered to be workers. They may be contracted by a large company such as a hotel or shopping mall or they may be sponsored individually by an Emirati family or by an Emirati–owned business.[4] Ranking higher on the scale are those who work in offices as clerks, secretaries and book-keepers. Still higher are the professional fields such as engineering, architecture, accounting and project management. At the top are financial advisors (there is a lot of money that needs investing), university professors and instructors, consultants, petroleum specialists and so forth. The top several layers of the hierarchy are divided ethnically/nationally and it is common to hear distinctions such as 'the Lebanese man in the office' or 'the Egyptian engineer' being made. When an Emirati refers to an 'Arab in the shop' this means any Arab other than an Emirati. Expatriate and its shortened version, expat, is used most commonly to denote foreigners who are non-Arab and non-South Asian; this means those from Europe, North and South America, Australia and New Zealand.[5] The laborers and workers are the most visible of the foreign populations because they are the most numerous. The streets of Abu Dhabi teem with them and 'other Arabs' and expats all of whom have come to the UAE with languages and dialects, cultural mores, clothing styles and expectations. They also come with ideas and impressions about the UAE and Emiratis. There is little if any interaction between Emiratis and laborers, and the expat population remains rather cut off from Emiratis as well. There are several reasons for this: separate residential areas, separate schools for expat children, separate clubs and social organizations. The social separation is not complete of course and does not imply that Emiratis are unaware of the expats around them or vice versa. In fact, Emiratis are keenly conscious that they are watched in the malls and other public places. For their part, expatriates are very curious about their hosts, but that curiosity is often wrapped in uninformed stereotypes. My introduction to life and work in Abu Dhabi is a good introduction to the expat point of view.

Arrival

All the glass surfaces at Abu Dhabi airport dripped with condensation at 3 o'clock in the morning. My glasses fogged over as I stepped out of the plane and onto the rolling stairway; I almost fell. It was so hot and the air so thick with humidity that I found it hard to breathe. Abu Dhabi is the hub of hell in August and that is when I arrived in 2001 as a new faculty member at Zayed University. The university was new, only three years old, and there were close to sixty people on the plane with me who would be joining the faculty as well. We were marched through passport control en masse and then waited for our bags on the oblong carousel. Tired from flying and stunned by the temperature and the humidity, we were not an imposing group. We would get to know each other in the days of orientation and settling in to our apartments in the weeks that followed. That night none of us had the energy to muster more than a limp smile.

In my mind Abu Dhabi was to be a homecoming of sorts. I grew up in Egypt and was happy to be returning to the Middle East. I half-expected Abu Dhabi to be a smaller, cleaner Cairo. I was in for a big surprise. Abu Dhabi was a brand new city; only one building was older than forty years. The wide main streets were planted with palms, hardy plants and grass that was manicured neatly. The smaller streets and back alleys of the city were less attractive. Some of the areas were crowded with cars and littered with garbage. Still, compared to the streets of Cairo this was paradise. At the end of a blitzkrieg first week of shopping for furniture, dishes, drapes, towels and appliances to set up my university assigned apartment, it suddenly dawned on me that I hadn't actually seen more than one or two Emiratis.[6]

'Locals? Oh, they'll all be in London now, no one stays in the summer.' Like Rome or Paris, I thought, but the shops were all open, the restaurants were full and the city seemed to be humming along. I was assured by veteran expatriates that it didn't make any difference if Emiratis were gone as they 'didn't do anything anyway.' That comment was my first sample of the expatriate view of Emiratis. The complete narrative goes something like this: 'They were just poor Bedouin before oil, no schools, nothing, and then suddenly

17

filthy rich and not a clue what to do. Foreigners built the place and they run it too. The only Emiratis you will see working will be tokens, there to make things look better. Women are all in those black things and they are only supposed to have oodles of kids.'

I carried with me another narrative about the Gulf and Gulf Arabs that I had absorbed from Egyptians. For my fellow graduates of the American University in Cairo in the late 1970s, getting a job in the Gulf was a prize that meant a much higher salary. The Gulf States were a draw for less educated Egyptians as well. Thousands of Egyptian men had flocked to the Emirates, Kuwait and Saudi Arabia to capitalize on the higher wages available there. The massive development projects undertaken in the late seventies and early eighties in these countries meant that there was no shortage of jobs in construction. The men had worked, spent little and sent as much money back to Egypt as they could. When they had accumulated enough or could no longer tolerate the separation from their family they returned home and used their savings to buy taxis, motorcycles, sewing machines—anything that would set them up in a small business. I had worked with some of these returned migrants in the late eighties when I was doing my dissertation research in Cairo (Bristol-Rhys 1987). Few that I can remember ever said anything positive about the Arabs of the Gulf. They talked about long working days, being duped with fines and fees, the humiliation of being treated like a slave and happiness that they were safely home. A few men who had been fired and forced to return to Egypt earlier than they had planned described Emiratis as capricious, hot-tempered and corrupt. These men were not skilled; they had been manual laborers, bricklayers, and construction site men who worked in the staggering heat day in and day out. The money they saved was earned by hard work in difficult conditions. This group had little direct contact with the Emirati population. Their supervisors and foremen were migrant workers like themselves. The lowest paid were bussed to and from their job sites and lived in labor camps on the outskirts of cities. They focused on what their sacrifice would allow them to do in Egypt where their real life would resume. Of the more than one hundred I interviewed, only three had returned for a second contract. As I remembered these conversations I wondered if I would make it through my full contract.

These perspectives that I remembered from Egypt jostled against what I was seeing. I had visited Abu Dhabi in 1973 on a business trip with my father.[7] The city now bore no resemblance to the sleepy little town it had been then. Abu Dhabi was a town then, not a city. The few buildings were clustered along the Gulf shore; there were a few hotels, banks, oil company offices, houses and squat three- and five-storey apartment blocks but not much more. Now the town had towering buildings, green parks and tree-lined boulevards and had grown into a sizeable city that expanded out to the edges of the island on which it sits. For a people who 'did nothing' this was pretty impressive. I set out to learn the history of the place.

In 2001 there was only one bona fide bookshop in Abu Dhabi and it really didn't have much to offer in English. The Emirati perspective on all the changes that had taken place was represented by two men, Al Gurg and Al Fahim, who wrote memoirs after the initial boom of development in the seventies and the rapid changes that transformed the city of Abu Dhabi and their lives (Al Fahim 1995; Al Gurg 1998). Their books still stand out because they are personal accounts, and much of the balance of the English language literature on the Emirates is academic and written by non-Emiratis. There are notable histories of the region, discussions of the effects of the British presence and, in fact, the exact nature of that presence, articles that examine how tribal allegiances were translated into wealth and status through appointments in the new and rapidly expanding government, the creation of the welfare bureaucracy that cares for citizens from cradle to grave, and now, more recently, the zealous efforts to preserve Emirati cultural heritage and strengthen Emirati identity.[8] There too is a collection of books written by expatriate women, some of whom were here before the wealth of oil, like Susan Hillyard and Gertrude Dyck (Dyck 1999; Hillyard 2002); one who worked here (Caesar 2002); and the story of the relationship between a British 'foster family' and that of the Emirati boy they mentored during his studies in London (Holton 1991).

I read through the University Library's collection and then moved on to the National Library. Finally I felt a little more comfortable about my historical knowledge and thought that I had a good grasp

19

of Emirati society. But I was apprehensive. How was I going to get along with 'rich and lazy' students? My students in New York had been economically disadvantaged and some recently paroled. This would certainly be a new experience.

The first thing I discovered about my students was that they knew no more than I did about the recorded history of their country, and in most cases much less. For young women in their late teens and early twenties, there was no history before 1971 when the separate ruled emirates joined together in a federation that was called the United Arab Emirates. These women were focused on the future, not the past. But in my mind, arrogant professor that I was, the past was important and they needed to know about it! I eventually began teaching a course on the heritage of the Emirates and that compelled me to research the traditions of Emirati culture. Many of the traditions had Bedouin origins, such as Nabati poetry, dance, falconry, camel breeding and racing, while the songs of the pearling boats and fishing lore were associated with the settled coastal communities. My students in those first years explored their past with me, and while they may not have become as enthusiastic as I would have liked, I was fascinated. What fascinated me and still does today is how Emiratis look at their history, their culture and their lives in the context of the amazing and swift changes brought by oil revenues that have altered the physical landscape of the country, brought in hundreds of thousands of foreigners and, in the short span of one generation, allowed people who were born in palm frond structures to fashion new lives and new identities in palatial villas in Abu Dhabi, London, Beirut and Geneva.

I started much of the ethnographic research presented here in 2001 as I began to learn about Emirati culture, history and society. My research has widened to include other topics over the years and narrowed sometimes to complete specific projects and articles. In 2002, with the launch of a project called *The Chronicles of Change*, I began collecting oral histories from Emirati women. Other specifically focused research has included Emirati weddings, historical narration, transnational migrants in the UAE, and how Emiratis are represented by a burgeoning tourist industry that is trying to promote the country's heritage. While undertaking research on those specific topics, I continued trying to understand the ways in which Emirati women, young and old, view their lives in the context of the changes that resulted from the discovery of oil.

The opinions, conversations and discussions presented here are taken from the accumulation of eight years of note-taking, interviews and participant observation conducted primarily in the emirate of Abu Dhabi. My research questions, and in fact often the topic chosen for research, bounced back and forth between my classes at Zayed University, where topics and themes were raised and discussed and then pursued with more formally organized question periods and interviews with other Emirati women. I have followed topics of discussion and inquiry raised in class, usually in response to changes in Abu Dhabi, such as the proposed new cultural institutions of the Guggenheim and the Louvre museums. I have also brought issues—like the treatment of migrant workers and runaway maids—to my classes for discussion and amplification. In these situations, while I am an alert observer, I am more a learning participant. Over the years in these classes we have explored just about every issue imaginable, some of which are included here.

It has been a balancing act to keep the component parts of my research 'field' distinct. This is especially true in the classroom environment where, given the roles of teacher and student, it has been crucial to maintain some distance as the students worked through their own research efforts. The students in my various classes know what 'I am working on' as they call it, and volunteer to read articles and chapters, and of course they insist on giving me a grade.

It is my good fortune and pleasure to be included in many of these young women's lives off campus as well, and their mothers, aunts, grandmothers and step-grandmothers have welcomed me into their families with open arms. All have taken great pains to answer my tedious questions, and we have discussed the topics that occupy them daily: children, cooking, life choices, religious beliefs, education, and plastic surgery, sex, diets, television shows, weddings and so on. Their willingness to speak candidly and sometimes emotionally about how their lives have changed, what they feel they have lost now, the importance of safeguarding traditions, and what they don't like about their new lives is a precious gift that has allowed me to understand Emirati society in ways that would have been impossible otherwise. It was and is the hours spent informally chatting, shopping and talking on the phone with Emirati friends that have allowed me to begin to understand and to appreciate the mix of restrictions, opportunities, challenges and disappointments that shape their lives. One of the benefits of living in Abu Dhabi and sharing my research with the women—young and old—who have helped to shape it is that they are all very personally involved. Nowadays, I don't even have to ask questions; my friends tell me what the 'next thing' is in Abu Dhabi and what I should be studying. There is still much to say.

Early in my research and explorations it became evident that each generation of Emirati women was articulating perspectives on their lives that were very different from the other generations but remarkably consistent within a generation. Older women spoke of loss, of forgetting and abandoning values and traditions. Their daughters talked about the new society that revolves around competitive displays of wealth and status. The younger women often called themselves the 'lost generation' because they thought that their lives would have no meaning.

It is the women's perceptions of their lives and the changes to Emirati society that I have used to organize the chapters in this book. Interviews and talks with women in their late sixties and seventies gave shape to 'Days of the Past' and their voices overlap with some of their daughters in 'Our New Lives Behind Walls'. Their daughters, in their forties and early fifties, talk of the new Emirati society that is wealthy and competitive in 'Tradition and Competition'. My students grapple with new opportunities and expectations that are often seen to be in conflict with cultural norms in 'Marriage, Education and Choices' and in 'Being Emirati Isn't Easy!' I begin by first describing the context in which these women live, and that is in a city and a country dominated by foreigners who have ideas about Emiratis and their lives. Maintaining discrete chapters has been somewhat difficult because conversations and discussions spill from one topic to another and so there is some overlap.

While the women I have talked with have all expressed their opinions quite openly, none wanted to be identified in the book, or indeed to be identifiable. I have therefore obscured identities throughout by omitting family names, using fictitious first names, altering locations of homes and compounds, and have in some cases blended individuals together. I can no longer recognize the women described here, so I am confident that no one else will be able to either.

One final preparatory note: the bulk of my research has been in the Emirate of Abu Dhabi, chiefly in the cities of Al Ain, Sha-hamma, Wathba and Abu Dhabi. Most of the changes that have occurred—rapid urbanization and development, influx of foreigners, the availability of domestic servants, tertiary education, access to medical services and consumer goods on an extraordinary level—have affected the whole country in varying degrees; and so while my work is grounded in Abu Dhabi, the prevailing theme of 'change' can be generalized to the other emirates. However, the wealth of Abu Dhabi residents, especially that in the city of Abu Dhabi, cannot be generalized to other cities or emirates. Abu Dhabi is one of the wealthiest cities in the world and the lifestyles enjoyed by Emiratis in this city are exceptional, even within a generally wealthy country. This is not to suggest that all Emiratis who live in the city of Abu Dhabi are millionaires, but many are and their houses, clothes, cars, jewelry and foreign real estate investments reflect that wealth. There are less wealthy families, to be sure, those who live what might be called middle-class lives. Of course, 'middle class' is a positional, relative term that often implies notions of social mobility and class aspiration as well as providing a rough estimate of family income. Characteristics that are assumed to be true of the American middle class, such as taxes, burdensome mortgages, the struggle to pay for college educations for their children and being bourgeois, do not apply to their Emirati counterparts. No one pays taxes, housing is often government supported and higher education is free. The connotations associated with middle class in the UAE are first economic: less money, probably earned through employment and not investment; and consequently less conspicuous display of consumer goods like cars, boats, watches, mobile phones and jewelry.

2

REPRESENTATIONS OF EMIRATIS

'We sometimes don't know who we are, and not knowing who we were doesn't help.'

It is hardly surprising that Emiratis are concerned about losing their cultural identity when globalization is physically manifested on city streets that teem with hundreds of thousands of transnational migrants. The national media provide extensive commentaries on the situation and report deepening worries that range from English supplanting Arabic in homes, plummeting morals, rising crime rates and evaporating cultural heritage, all of which are attributed to the presence of large numbers of foreigners. Local newspapers consistently identify all criminals by their nationality, so for instance we know that 'MK, a Pakistani' was the offender. While foreign migrant labor is blamed for nearly all social ills—robbery, drugs and prostitution—an expanding tourist industry vigorously markets the country as the new, ultimate destination for foreign tourists. One integral part of the plan to encourage tourism is to develop a heritage industry that will promote Emirati traditions and material culture. The other is to import arts and cultural institutions such as the Louvre and the Guggenheim to draw visitors, and, following the Dubai Development Model, to construct luxurious residential complexes that capitalize on the winter sun and placid Gulf waters and make those available for foreign purchase (Davidson 2007). The design and construction, as well as the continued maintenance of these developments, will all rely on the work of foreign migrants, but that is rarely mentioned. These two efforts, heritage and real estate, though connected in brochures and videos produced for the tourist industry, are quite incongruous and seem to be on distant ends of a continuum stretching from the noble but poor and desert-ravaged Bedouin to an ultra-modern, global city in which foreigners predominate and Emiratis are largely invisible. They are not only invisible in the future; Emiratis are often hard to find in history.

Photographers, Explorers and Expatriates

On my first visit to an Abu Dhabi bookstore, the clerk was a bit stumped when I asked him to point me to the section on Emirati history; but after thinking for a minute he smiled encouragingly and said, 'Yes, the picture books.' He led me to a display rack mounted on the back wall of the ground floor. They were indeed picture books: glossy, coffee-table size books of photographs taken of people and places in the country by two photographers, Noor Ali Rashid and Ronald Codrai (Codrai 1998a; 1998b; 2001; Rashid 1997a; 1997b; 1998). Rashid is considered the official photographer for the ruling families and his published works are subtitled 'The Royal Collection.' Codrai, after service in World War II and a posting in Cairo, came to the Trucial States in 1948 with D'Arcy Oil Concessions, a group that would soon be known as British Petroleum.

On the shelves below these photography books that capture images of the pre-oil past and the beginning of the development and growth were an odd assortment of paperbacks. Here was Wilfred Thesiger's *Arabian Sands* and, rather more intriguingly, his *Danakil Diaries* and *The Marsh Arabs* (1959; 1983; 1998). Nestled in the midst of these were Lane's *Manner and Customs of Modern Egyptians* and one lonely copy of Wehr's *Arabic Dictionary* (Lane 1890; Wehr 1994). Had I fallen down an orientalist rabbit hole?[1] Thesiger embodied for me the disaffected young man, stifled by English society, who had sought freedom, adventure and the exotic in lands far from home, but only those safely administered by compatriots who could always be relied upon for help, the odd survey job to tide one over, bath and fresh kit and an evening meal with the ladies. Thesiger started his career in a Sudan governed by the Condominium that was much more Anglo than Egyptian, moved on to Yemen to track locusts, and there, in the desert sands, far away from kith and kin, finds true friendship with his Bedouin guides. Thesiger's travels in Arabia lengthened and he crossed the peninsula several times, including a trek through the Empty Quarter, a place that sane men and camels avoid but which for him was a must-do. Thesiger was given the sobriquet 'Mubarak bin London,' blessed son of London, by his Omani companion guides. During his travels Thesiger crossed through the Trucial States, avoiding on one trip some fighting between Dubai and Abu Dhabi, and ultimately Thesiger met Sheikh Zayed, who became the first president of the country in 1971. At the time of their meeting Sheikh Zayed was governing the town of Al Ain and the cluster of oases around it. A faded black and white picture of Thesiger is displayed proudly with other notables on a wall in one of the old forts in Al Ain. A permanent exhibit of the photographs taken by Thesiger during his Arabian Peninsula travels is on display at the restored Al Jahili Fort in Al Ain.

Thesiger was every bit the intrepid traveler and deservedly famous for his books, and so it was at least somewhat understandable to find his titles in what was passing for a history section. However, travel writing is not history, not even when done by Thesiger, and it was all the more remarkable that his was the only text on the country. What Lane's book on Egypt was doing in the 'local interest' section I never established, but I did find Heard-Bey's comprehensive history on the country upstairs in the shop (1982). Two days later a new Emirati acquaintance presented me with Muhammad Abdullah's history of the UAE (1978) and I busied myself reading. I reckoned the odd assortment of titles in the 'local interest' section of the bookshop was due to the vagaries of retailing and thought no more about it until I was confronted once again with *Arabian Sands* and worse a week later.

An Emirati man who had recently retired from his government job asked me what I knew about the country. I told him that I had read Heard-Bey and Abdullah and that I found it intriguing to learn how much of the history of the country was to be found in the British records of their two hundred plus years in the region. 'Who?' he asked. 'Historians? Afraid I haven't read them; Emiratis don't much like history, especially if it's in English. And as for the British, they didn't do anything much until they helped us find oil in the late 50s,' he continued. I was a bit stunned that so much history was being swept under the rug and asked about the British treaties that forbade the rulers any dealings of any sort with any power other than the Crown. 'Nothing in that,' he told me; 'there was nothing to deal with before oil so no one cared.' Stunned again, I didn't want to argue with him about the history of his country on my third week in town so I was silent.

I was introduced to a few more Emiratis in the days that followed but met many more 'expats' amongst the British, American, Indian, French, Egyptian, Lebanese and about 150 other nationalities.[2] From that group I heard two narratives repeatedly. 'They were just Bedouins, really.' 'They had a few camels and goats, some date palms in Al Ain, but they were poor, very poor and then suddenly rich beyond belief.' 'Amazed they do so well; they had nothing whatsoever before oil and now look at the place! Fountains and trees, roads and palaces, skyscrapers, hotels and still they are building.' 'Crafty old pirates they are, in their blood I think, notorious for paying late, if at all.' 'Oh, a few are educated, sent abroad mostly, lots of those in the oil trade, trained up in the North Sea area, the rest I guess are in the government as that seems to be where they all end up.' 'Hard to get to know them, they don't much socialize with us, rather stand-offish you might say, probably because they don't like being around alcohol.' 'You know there was a slave market in Buraimi right up until the seventies?' 'Read *Arabian Sands*, have you? That will give you a good taste of what the Bedouin were like.' 'And Henderson, have you read his book? He was here at the very beginning, you know; wife still lives here, somewhere. You should read that one too [see Henderson 1988].' I smiled attentively but I knew that Emiratis had not all been pirates or 'just Bedouins' and that 'the beginning' was a long time before oil.

There are quite varied perceptions of and representations made about Emiratis, the land they inhabit, the life lived before oil and, indeed, what they are capable of doing in the future.

Emirati History

The principal historical records of the Emirates are British. These records are composed of thousands of pages of documents that were produced as the bureaucratic corollary of Britain's long presence in the Gulf. They document first the relationships with the individual rulers in the area, then with somewhat coalesced rulers who had all agreed to the same treaties that gave the area the name the Trucial States, and finally with the oil concessions and privileged position given to British banks, planning and construction companies in the 1960s and 70s as the new country built urban centers and the infrastructure to support growth and development (Hawley 1970:242; Kazim 2000:196, 210, 276; Tuson 2003:29)

The British documents, also commonly referred to as the Public Records, the Bombay Archives and the British Records, depending on the time period to be studied, contain official memos, minutes, instructions, maps, the compendium of tribes and their origins known as *Lorimer's Gazetteer*, and the personal letters and diaries of the men, and sometimes comments about their wives especially if they proved to be worrisome to the authorities, who served in the navy, Colonial Office or Foreign Office and were posted in the region (Tuson 2003:17, 30, 33).[3] Collectively these historical documents are somewhat troublesome if not problematic because they are far from value-neutral, and in many cases the tone is bluntly pejorative and condescending. Descriptions of 'the natives' and their rulers are a mixture of derision, gross ethnocentrism and downright scorn. Barbarians and pirates were among the most popular terms used, with the label 'pirate' writ large to encompass the lower Gulf as 'the Pirate Coast.' Of course, it might as easily be argued that the British were the piratical force in the Gulf waters, as they boarded the vessels of the Qawasim, the predominant tribal group of the northern Emirates, shot cannon balls at anchored ships and ultimately destroyed the economy of the coast, all to fur-

29

ther their own interests and, some contend, to take over the rather lucrative trade that the Qawasim controlled (Al Qasimi 1986; cf Davies 1997). However, the label 'the Pirate Coast' does underscore the fact that the British focus was on the coastal regions while the interior, which appeared to offer nothing but sand, was ignored and the inhabitants dismissed as Bedouin.

Piracy was not the only illegal activity that the British identified and then sought to eradicate. The rulers of the lower Gulf were also labeled slave traders and were made to sign an anti–slaving treaty in 1838 (Kazim 2000:142). To what extent ships under the control of these rulers actually did engage in conveying slaves remains unclear, and Emiratis have told me that the household slaves in the area had been transported by Omanis who dominated the slave trade in the area. This fine distinction did not deter the newly minted humanitarian enthusiasm with which the British outlawed slavery, and the rulers of Ras al Khaimah, Ajman, Dubai and Abu Dhabi all signed the agreement presented to them which permitted their ships to be boarded if slaves were suspected (Burnett 2006). Now ships could be detained, boarded and searched on suspicion of piracy and slavery, and the waters of the Gulf were totally con- trolled by the British (Kazim 2000:144).

The many personal letters and diaries of Britons who came to the area are fascinating, and they offer a glimpse into the society of British travelers and workers as colonial and foreign office officials. Women's letters and diaries show concern with the relative merits of various postings, proper entertaining and setting up domestic arrangements (Hillyard 2002; Tuson 2003:84). The Trucial States were considered a hardship posting, though several thought it pref- erable to being in India (Tuson 2003:50). The letters also demon- strate the propensity to employ words learned in other imperial lands such as 'durbar' and 'jirga' for a large and important meeting and, of course, the ubiquitous 'wallah' used to refer to any male servant (Jacob 2007:64; Tuson 2003:43). There is a sense in these narratives that much is interchangeable, natives are natives no mat- ter what language they speak, but, as one woman advised, it is best when possible to 'bring Indians with you as domestic servants because they, after all, have been properly trained' (Tuson 2003:35).

No serious attempt was made, it seems, to convince an Emirati to work in a *memsahib*'s house. In fact, there is little mention of the natives of the Trucial States in documents written in the early 1900s. There was little interaction between the British of both genders with all but the rulers and their immediate representatives.

Others, outside of the colonial/protectorate/oil paradigm, wrote as well. We have the travels and memories of Hermann Burckhardt, a German traveler and photographer whose photographs taken in 1903 provide fascinating glimpses into the rule of one of the most powerful sheikhs on the Trucial Coast, Sheikh Zayed bin Khalifa, commonly known in Abu Dhabi as Zayed the First and Zayed the Great. Zwemer was a missionary closely associated with missions established in Bahrain and Oman. His writing is laced with evangelical zeal and grave concern for the lost souls of Arabia. The reports and letters home published in the mission publications, *Neglected Arabia* and *Arabia Calling*, would be used to raise money to support their work in Arabia (Zwemer 1902; 1988). Later his mission successors would establish a hospital in Al Ain with permission granted by Sheikh Shakhbut bin Sultan al Nahayan, the ruler of Abu Dhabi, who was apparently justifiably confident that the missionaries would have little success converting his subjects. A young Canadian nurse, Gertrude Dyck, responded to the mission call and arrived in Al Ain in 1962 to work at the newly established hospital. She stayed for over forty years. Her memoirs of life in Al Ain, published in the UAE, make no mention of the mission connection or proselytizing (Dyck 1999).

The Days of Harsh Nobility

Later, when the Trucial States had amalgamated into an independent and oil-rich United Arab Emirates, the diary-writing genre is superseded by 'I was there' accounts of the harsh and impoverished life lived before the discovery of oil. Most of these were written by individuals who had some official capacity that brought them to the country. Edward Henderson, who wrote two such accounts, was in 1948 an employee of Petroleum Development Trucial Coast, and then in 1956 he entered the British Foreign

Service and continued to serve in the region (Henderson 1988; 1999). Hawley, who now is often cited as an historian and has indeed written a very good history of the area, was Her Majesty's Political Resident from 1958 to 1961 (Hawley 1970). Ronald Codrai, who used a camera rather than a pen, was, as the saying goes, an oil man. His photographs taken from the 1940s are in some cases the only ones on record (Codrai 1998b; 2001). Then there is of course the famous Thesiger whom I have previously mentioned. He conveniently provides a clear exposition of the particular perspective evinced by most of the foreigners who have written accounts of the pre-oil days.

Thesiger despised any and all development that would change his beloved Arabia, and most especially the Bedouin life that he had come to appreciate and which he guarded ferociously. On his last visit to the UAE before his death, he grumbled and complained incessantly about the roads, buildings, air conditioning, cars and congestion that had transformed the desert into so much modernity (Gardner 2003). For Thesiger, it seems, oil had ruined the land and the people, with the very notable exception of his great friend, Sheikh Zayed bin Sultan al Nahayan. Thesiger's perspective that honor and nobility reside only in the desert echoes Ibn Khaldun's judgment that the settled life, the city life, is ruinous (Khaldun 1958). While some Emiratis have expressed similar thoughts when they survey the bustling cities that have grown up in the last four decades, few—if any—consider that they have Bedouin desert traditions to return to and cannot imagine life without the amenities and conveniences provided by development.

The young female Emiratis who are my students speak of the past with a romanticized nostalgia that is fed by the constructed and often air-brushed images broadcast on local television stations, particularly during Ramadan. As romantic as the past can be made to appear, few have any illusion about the hard life lived by their grandparents. The older Emiratis to whom I have spoken, those who lived in the 1940s and '50s, talk about how hard life was and mention the small industries, like firewood, charcoal, chickens, goats and vegetables, that allowed them to survive.

Words and Pictures: Representations of Emiratis

What are 'the natives' like, then? From the primarily British historical records it might be taken that Emiratis are either pirates who
sometimes dabbled in the slave trade or else nomadic Bedouin.
Happily the piracy and slavery labels have fallen away, but perhaps
only because a minority of new arrivals delve into the history of the
country. What has remained is perhaps more dangerous, however.
This is a highly romanticized and stylized representation of Emirati
life before oil, when all men had a falcon on their wrist, coffee bub-
bled on the campfire and life was simple and honest. The photographs of Codrai and Thesiger especially are important in this
constructed image of simplicity in the desert, and though Rashid's
pictures are more formally composed and usually taken within a
building, his too show austere, noble faces framed by *'gutra*, the
flowing head-cloth worn by men. Photographs published by Dyck
and more recently Hillyard do show Emiratis in towns with houses
and buildings, but they too convey a sense of honorable innocence
as men and sometimes women stare directly into the camera (Dyck
1999; Hillyard 2002).

Most expatriates, and now an increasing number of tourists, are
presented with an array of images and tourist souvenirs that depict
Bedouin life. The image of the noble Arab living a life of admirable
poverty in the harsh desert is displayed in a variety of ways
throughout the cities of the UAE in shops, hotels, media and adver-
tisements. Camels are a favorite if over-used symbol, found on
tourist bumper stickers, note cards or placemats, and are fashioned
from leather, glass, pottery and cut crystal adorned with gemstones.
Falcons compete with the ubiquitous camel, and adorn ashtrays,
t-shirts and inlaid boxes. *Dallah*, the graceful coffeepot, comes in a
variety of sizes and substances like brass, silver and gold. These are
the 'desert heritage collection' of memorabilia for sale that often
include a miniature 'Bedouin camp' complete with tents, cooking
fire and resting camels that can be purchased as fridge magnets or
as stand-alone *tableaux vivants* in a variety of sizes.

Emirati national dress, composed of the white *kandoura* for men
worn with the *'gutra* head-cover that is secured with the black *agal*,

33

and the women's black *'abayah* and *shaylah*, are reproduced in some rather tasteless ways as well. Salt and pepper shakers, representing an Emirati man and woman, are marketed as 'Sheikh and Sheikha.' Corpulent porcelain 'Arabs' in national dress are sold as money banks, and successively smaller 'sheikhs' are stacked as nesting dolls.

Emiratis find these trinkets and souvenirs disconcerting and insulting. A new stylized fridge magnet that depicts a woman in national dress pushing a full shopping cart captioned 'shopping is an acceptable profession' they consider particularly demeaning. They find little comfort in the fact that the same goods are sold in Doha, Kuwait City and Manama. Those of my students who have visited Muscat protest that the Omanis don't have to put up with such insensitive and ridiculous images 'because they have a credible heritage industry.'

As irritating and embarrassing as the crass tourist merchandise is, my students complain more about what they call the Bedouin myth. Few think of themselves as 'Bedouin' and just as few consider their families to have been so in the past. Most of their families lived in towns, Abu Dhabi, Dubai, Sharjah and Al Ain, and the Bedouin life has little resonance for them. I do have students who number among the families who were 'settled' into *buyut as-shaabiyya*, the houses built for the Bedouin back in the late 1960s, but that is ancient history as far as they are concerned and has little meaning for their lives today. The announcement in 2007 that the Abu Dhabi Authority for Culture and Heritage was planning to build a Bedouin Museum was met with skepticism and derision. Although many Emiratis may appreciate the fact that the hype and marketing of their 'Bedouin-ness' is just that, there are others who do not, and the stereotypical image of the Arab in the desert has some significantly negative connotations. The fact that it is government agencies, such as Abu Dhabi's Authority for Culture and Heritage, that promote such imagery is somewhat confounding.

As previously mentioned, one commonly heard expatriate comment about Emiratis is that they are lazy and, beyond that, completely ill-suited for work. 'Emiratis are just lazy; they have never had to work, you know, so they don't know how.' 'They didn't have a thing before oil, and if it had been up to them the blasted stuff would still be in the ground! No way could they have gotten it out without us.' In this last quote there is a bit of truth, as the Emirati population in the 1960s had little technical training or the specific skills necessary to launch a petro-chemical industry. It is the frank innuendo of lazy haplessness that I wish to address here, an insinuation that Emiratis are incapable in some essential way because they were poor Bedouin. This is, of course, not only patently false but rests upon the erroneous presupposition that Bedouin life, even if poor, was predicated upon ease, leisure and the carefree notions of the noble savage living in nature. While we all know that to be ludicrous, the idea has permeated into the expatriate narrative in the UAE with remarkable resilience. I have heard it repeated by people who have just arrived in the country and by those who have resided here for decades; by professional, corporate officers, university professors, their children and even relatives visiting them. My Emirati students tell me they are aware that people think they are lazy and incapable of working. This troubles them greatly, but many say they have heard it so frequently they too have come to believe it. Discussions about the reasons why Emiratis consider certain jobs entirely unacceptable usually end with 'but we don't want to work, we want jobs in offices that are comfortable and clean and we want to draw big salaries.' Students also point out they have never seen an Emirati doing manual labor unless it is their grandfather puttering around with his palm trees. Manual and service work, for now two generations of Emiratis, has been work done exclusively by foreigners. With media coverage of the high priority given to Emirati employment through implementation of the Emiratization policy, this stereotypical representation is being challenged somewhat. What are not being challenged are the stylized, romanticized and mistaken perceptions about the nature of Emirati society before oil that feed the stereotype. The 'natives' were not all Bedouin; in fact, it was primarily only in the interior of Abu Dhabi emirate where tribes were nomadic; permanent settlements were on the coast, in the mountains and near oases. And there was nothing romantic or leisurely about anyone's life: even the rulers suffered from lack of water, shortages of food, harsh weather and poverty. The constructed image of the noble Bedouin gazing serenely into the distant sands may be used to underpin the tourist industry, but it does no favors to the Emiratis who must contend with expatriates who believe that the 'natives' are rather useless.

Tourism: Building a Strange Future

This constructed image of the noble Bedouin looking out over pristine dunes in the desert is rather oddly brought to life for tourists through various activities. There are tours of so-called 'heritage villages' to see tents, camels and falcons. Dune-bashing trips in the desert are advertised heavily in tourist brochures and through hotel concierges. These 'desert safari' adventures are a day in the desert that includes a ride on a camel, several runs up impossibly high dunes in a comfortable 4x4, Bedouin tents, a barbeque and, to finish off the day, a belly dancer. This is the tourists' Bedouin experience. No one to whom I spoke could explain, much less justify, the belly dancer but I was assured that 'everyone expected one.' More adventurous tourists can spend the night in the desert and experience Bedouin life by sleeping in permanent tents pitched on concrete pads and having to tiptoe across the sand to reach plumbed and completely modern bathroom facilities.

There are tourist excursions to other sites as well, and some of the heritage villages do depict settled life in the oases and on the coast. Sadly these heritage attractions fall into one of two categories: forlorn or fantasy. The forlorn villages are often in need of a thorough cleaning, and the mats, cushions and baskets displayed are frayed, badly arranged and presented without interpretation or explanation. The fantasy villages and sites mix a romanticized past with a technologically dependent present under the guise of 'old.' The traditional, such as old Indian-style beds and charcoal braziers, are displayed in rooms that are barely five years old and have power outlets, air conditioning and, in one particularly bizarre setting, an Emirati automaton who waves and greets visitors.

Tourists seek authenticity but rarely find it, and the link between tourism and cultural heritage is often a tenuous one. This is especially true in the UAE as the governments of the individual Emirates invest heavily in tourism as an alternative to petro-chemicals, in the case of Abu Dhabi, and to add new revenue streams to the economies of Dubai and the smaller, oil-challenged Emirates. The issues of heritage, history and representation are a part of public discourse with daily commentary in the newspapers, conferences on Emirati identity and history, and television programming that glorifies the pre-oil past while advertisers market real estate in a very post-modern future. The cultural and arts district being constructed on Saadiyat, an island adjacent to Abu Dhabi, has become the lightning rod for Emiratis who find much that is objectionable in the Frank Gehry and Zaha Hadid architectural designs that are destined to be the city's new icons. Variously phrased, the objections all convey the notion that there is a remarkable lack of resonance with the physicality of Saadiyat in all the connotations associated with that word—size, color, shape, layout, location, design and motif. The complexes of buildings that will anchor the new cultural district are distinctively post-modern, as one would expect from Gehry and Hadid. As depicted in scale model, they create a built environment that is rather foreboding and quite alien to the desert island on which they will be built.[4]

The model for the entire island, complete with palm trees to scale, is on display at the Emirates Palace Hotel and I take my students to see it whenever possible. Most of these young women, it must be said, are thrilled to be able to visit the hotel because hotels, even those as grand and expensive as the Palace, are strictly off-limits for most Emirati women and so many visit the gold-leafed marvel for the first time on one of our class trips. They like the design of the hotel, which might be described as modern Ottoman. Their eyebrows sometimes rise higher as each successively less clothed tourist walks by us, and they usually express the feeling that the hotel is foreign and that they feel as if they have left the UAE. In many ways they have. There are few Emiratis to be seen and those that are present are men, usually clustered in the café area where they meet with foreign businessmen, drink coffee with friends and watch the parade of tourists. My students are very wary of being seen by other Emiratis in this environment because their presence in a hotel, even on a chaperoned fieldtrip, may be sufficient to set off a round of malicious gossip. Hotels are viewed by many with suspicion and distrust, primarily because of the availability of alcohol and the close proximity of bedrooms. The UAE is a Muslim country and alcohol is therefore forbidden; however, concessions have been made for non-Muslim foreigners who may drink alcohol. Hotels and private clubs are the only venues at which alcohol may be served. Alcohol may be purchased for consumption in one's home at licensed liquor shops and one should possess a personal liquor license, issued by the emirate, to be allowed to purchase. Hotels may pour freely and do; cocktail lounges and bars are prominent, as are nightclubs. For most of my students, and it seems for all of their parents, just the fact that some people might be consuming alcohol nearby is cause for concern. Some, of course, are much more relaxed about alcohol and don't mind eating in a restaurant where it is served or dining with non-Muslim acquaintances who have wine with their meal.

All of the students wear a *shaylah*, the headscarf that is worn to cover the hair and neck, but few wrap it so that is obscures the face unless we come across Emirati men. Then, in a flurry of fabric and hands, they quickly adjust their scarves to bring one length of the scarf up over the back of the head so that it drapes down over the face. The scarf fabric is thin enough for the person wearing it to see through it but it completely hides the face when viewed from any distance. The students have learned to watch out for pushy tourists who try to take photographs and videos of them walking across the lobby. 'I don't want to end up on YouTube or worse!' Seldom do tourists try to engage any of us in conversation.

On a fieldtrip to the National Museum in Al Ain, the historical oasis city located inland from Abu Dhabi, one woman tourist stumbled into interaction with the students. On this fieldtrip the students' assignment was to assess the effectiveness of the museum critically based on several factors: display aesthetics, interpretation, education, historical accuracy and their overall impression of the museum. They busied themselves with their assignment by scrutinizing the dioramas, display cases, information cards, lighting and general facilities. Their observations sadly were far from positive.

We gathered in a small room just off the main lobby to discuss their assessments. The room in which we gathered had been designed to resemble the inside of a tent by covering the walls with traditional woven black and red wool. The floor was laid with carpets while low cushions and bolsters created seating against the walls. We were engaged immediately in a rather loud discussion of what was wrong with the museum, from the very fundamental need for a rigorous cleaning to the factual mistakes and translation errors on information cards. Most of the students were not happy that the dressed mannequins which displayed traditional clothes were not only covered with dust, but they looked far from Arab and, in fact, might have been taken from a department store in London and then had the faces darkened with a substance looking suspiciously like shoe polish. One of the students was very angry about this. 'We spend millions to bring modern art here and millions more to build fancy hotels and yet this is the best we can do with our own heritage.' Engrossed in discussion about the need for accurate representation, we didn't notice that we had attracted attention. 'Excuse me!' blurted Noor as she noticed suddenly that a woman holding a camera was crouched down in front of her. 'What are you doing?' I stood up and took two quick steps that put me between the camera and the two students it was pointed at. 'Excuse me, it is considered very rude to take pictures of people without asking permission.' The woman reacted with shock. 'But I thought this was a display and I wanted some close-ups!' She reddened with embarrassment. 'No, this is no display, these are real, live Emirati university students.' She brightened and looked around at the fifteen young women. 'Oh my goodness! We have been visiting the country for several days now and we haven't actually seen any Emiratis.' She hesitated for a moment and then asked me if she could talk to the students. 'Of course you can talk to us, you just can't take pictures,' the answer came like a chorus from around the room. The students fielded her questions with gracious diplomacy, allowed her to take pictures of the henna tracery on the hands of two who had been to a recent wedding, and explained that it was caution about pictures being shared on the internet that made them concerned, not because of a belief that the camera stole their souls. She was amazed to learn that they were university students since she didn't think women were educated 'in the desert' and seemed quite disappointed when no one could talk about the camels she thought were tethered in all villa gardens. The woman's husband came looking for her and we were quite amused when she ordered him out of the room because it was the 'women's harem' and no men were permitted.

On the drive home to Abu Dhabi we discussed this interaction and the museum within the context of what both told us about the tourist experience in the UAE, representations of Emiratis and notions of authenticity. All had been reading widely in the literature on heritage and tourism and so were conversant with the concept of the tourist gaze, the search for authenticity and the manufacturing of heritage (Alsayyad 2001; Coleman and Crang 2002; Crouch and Lubbren 2003; Rojek and Urry 1997; Shaw and Williams 2004; Smith 2006; Urry 2002). For all of the students that day, representation and authenticity were troublesome. In fact, other than the very clearly authentic archaeological artifacts on display at the museum, they felt that authenticity had been abandoned entirely. The museum's representations of Emiratis were, for the students, the least authentic. One pointed out that while there was a single display that featured a water well and one other that depicted a woman weaving, there were hundreds of guns and falconry gear displayed in cases throughout the museum and this, to her mind, created a very false impression of Emirati lives in the pre-oil past.

A voice rose from the back of the bus. 'Maybe inauthentic is in fact Emirati authentic!' This fired up everyone's imagination. 'We are brand-name conscious because we think that means authentic good taste; and we import designers and planners to build our cities because we don't want to look authentic, we want to look modern and Western.' And from another, 'But now we want tourists to come and spend money here and so we are being packaged as Bedouins even though that is far from authentic.'

The notions of authenticity and representation are likely to stimulate more discussion as the tourist industry continues to develop. While my students may be critical of what they are seeing on display now in museums and gift shops, they readily admit that they would not be aware of such things if they had not gone as part of a class. Historical accuracy will require historical knowledge, and that is sadly lacking among a great portion of the Emirati population.

3

DAYS OF THE PAST

Patience and Poverty

There are but a few souls still living who remember the extreme poverty that settled on the people of Abu Dhabi in 1929 when the pearl market bottomed out. The global economic depression drastically reduced demand for luxury goods, and accordingly the demand for Gulf pearls suffered. If that was not bad enough, the second blow was Japan's success in cultivating pearls that were readily available and much cheaper than the hard-won pearls brought up by divers in the Gulf. Abu Dhabi had been quite a prosperous small town up until 1929, but it soon dwindled as houses were abandoned and people moved away—back to families in the oasis areas, to relatives in Dubai and Doha, and anywhere else where fortunes might be fairer. The houses built by the pearl merchant families began to crumble and the town's markets faltered and closed down, leaving just one that was sadly under-stocked for the remaining inhabitants (Lienhardt 2001:118). Abu Dhabi would not change much for the next twenty years, but in the early 1950s there was talk that oil might be found—after all, it had been found in Qatar and Saudi Arabia; the people of Abu Dhabi hoped that it would be found sooner rather than later.

By the late 1950s the search for oil deposits intensified and there was optimism that it would be found. No one then could have imagined how their lives would be transformed in one short decade. Abu Dhabi town, eponymous with the island upon which it sits and the territorial borders of the emirate, was a rather destitute, ramshackle collection of palm frond houses that radiated out from the one building of substance, Qasr al Hosn, the rulers' fort. Poverty hung like a dark cloud. There were no roads, no electricity, no medical help, and potable water was desperately scarce outside the oases and was often brought in oil drums from Dubai, Qatar and across the Gulf from Persia and further up the coast (Heard-Bey 1982:237; Lienhardt 2001:114). From these historical and anthropological accounts we know that Abu Dhabi in the 1950s was an unimposing settlement and that life must have been rather miserable. I had all but given up hope of meeting any women who remembered those days clearly when a student, Hend, told me that she knew an old woman who would be happy to talk to me. Hend arranged for me to be driven to the house where the woman lived with her daughter, Anood.

'God was merciful in those times.' Maryam's comment startled me. Maryam is nearly eighty years old. She has outlived her husband by twenty years now. Saif died of kidney disease. That is a common health problem among the population of older Emirati because in their younger years there was not only a lack of water, but the water that was available was brackish, high in salts and sometimes tainted. Maryam suffers from the same disease and goes for dialysis regularly, but never have I heard her complain about the procedure or the pain. Her daughter, Anood, hovers around us as we talk because she is very concerned that Maryam will tire quickly. Maryam shoos Anood away with her hand. '*Binti*, either sit down and relax or go to the kitchen. I can't think with you moving about like a nurse.' Anood pretends to go to the kitchen but she stops in the hallway just out of her mother's sight. 'Yes, merciful,' Maryam says again. 'We had no idea what was happening in other places; we didn't know that other people took hospitals for granted, we didn't know the whole world wasn't poor like us.' We talk about how Abu Dhabi had been in her youth. 'You know, I smile every time I go into the toilet here in this house! Every time! Because I always remember that we had to use the beach when I was young. Can you imagine? It is true, the beach that we like to call the Corniche now, that was the toilet for everyone.' Maryam shakes her head at the memory. 'We women only went down at night, of course. The darkness gave us some privacy at least. During the day it was hard and we would look for spots that were hidden, like behind the low scrubby bushes.' She stopped then for a moment or two and was silent. 'But, you know, we managed okay and since everyone lived that way we didn't really think about it too much. I remember that I was always thirsty though. Always I was thirsty.' Anood reappears with herbal tea for her mother and coffee for me. Maryam pulls her daughter's arm and makes her sit on the couch. 'I remember my mother talking about the water machine that was in the *Ingleezi* house.' I asked if she meant Susan Hillyard, the first British woman to live in Abu Dhabi. 'Yes, the woman with the little girl. They had a machine that made drinking water from bad water. It was magic and everyone talked about it. We didn't know such a machine could exist.' Hillyard mentions in her book that many women came to taste the distilled water, so many in fact that she had to ration it (Hillyard 2002:26). I told Maryam what Susan said about women drinking the sweet water. 'Yes, yes, I was one of those! It was at the time when those *Ingleezi* came that we started to see other things, to learn about the rest of the world. Can you imagine how much worse it would have been if we had known? God kept us separated and isolated out of mercy.'

Maryam is probably right that Abu Dhabi's isolation had been merciful, but perhaps not entirely divine; the British do get some credit too. Beginning in the late 1700s with the East India Company's efforts to safeguard its Indian resources and, crucially, one of the shipping routes from India, until 1971 when Britain announced that it would withdraw from the Gulf, British interests had dominated the region. In fact, the small emirates or states were known collectively as the Trucial States in reflection of the multiple treaties that had established British hegemony and maintained it by virtue of clauses that forbade any ruler from having contact or contract with any entity—sovereign or corporate—that was not British. They called this protection, and therefore the UAE celebrates not independence but the metamorphosis from Protectorate to nation-state on 2 December.

There are many perspectives on the British dealings with the seven emirates that eventually became the United Arab Emirates. Not surprisingly, the fact that oil was discovered by a British consortium has had the effect of stifling what might have been a mostly critical assessment. Indeed, much of the pre-oil history of Abu Dhabi is ignored and younger Emiratis are often unaware of the long-term British naval presence and so they speak only about the British finding oil. I will return to this particular historical narrative, but regarding the isolation imposed, whether divine or diabolical, the majority of the population in the pre-oil years would never have seen a representative of British imperial interests. Britain maintained ships in the Gulf, necessary to gunboat diplomacy, hired non-native agents to conduct affairs on land, paid rulers for various uses of their land, like aircraft landing, weighed in with force during factional disputes within ruling families and even agreed to the secession of one or two of those factions, but rarely if ever came ashore (Onley 2004; 2005). This was a policy of non-intervention, and while it allowed for payments to rulers (pittances that they were) and stepping in when needed to promote British interests, as they were defined, it conveniently prevented the British from initiating any projects that might have benefited the local population until very late in their tenure.[1]

In Abu Dhabi the situation was made worse by the fact that Sheikh Shakhbut, who ruled from 1928 to 1966, apparently harbored an extraordinary distrust of the British. Reading through the Records of the Emirates, it is clear that anything proposed by the British Sheikh Shakhbut would veto, anything they supported he rejected, and even when cajoled he would prevaricate long enough to kill the idea (Tuson 1990). Consequently, while the people of Dubai were benefiting from their ruler's less prickly relationship with the British, the political residency was transferred to Dubai in 1954, which quickly began to capitalize on trade and commerce, while Abu Dhabi stagnated (Abdullah 1978:134).

Miya, mish zeit! Water, not oil!

Egyptians celebrate the spring holiday of Shem al Nessim, during which one is supposed to 'smell the springtime,' literally. With eyes crinkled and great laughs, older Emirati women say that here, in the months before the long sought after oil was finally found, that you could '*shem az-zeit*', smell the oil. The smell of oil was in the air and also the excitement of what would happen when, *in sha'allah*, it was found. For although few Emiratis knew what was involved in oil prospecting, geological surveys, test wells or anything of the elaborate and highly technical processes that would turn this buried treasure into something that they could actually use, everyone had heard about what had happened in Kuwait, Saudi Arabia and Qatar after oil was discovered. Oil would make life better. Discontent over the persistent harshness of life had been bubbling up. Stories and rumors of doctors, hospitals and schools elsewhere, as close as Dubai, made the people of Abu Dhabi wonder when their lives would improve. The fact that the material goods trickling into the *suq* (market), such as fabrics, ammunition, farming tools and even drinking water, were coming from Dubai did not go unnoticed.

'We waited, but not easily, it must be said.' Umm Hamad is in her early seventies and her hands, obscured partially by huge sparkling diamond rings, are big and her knuckles are pronounced, like my grandmother's had been, showing not only age but also the ravages of years of hard work. 'What we really wanted was water and medical treatment. If oil could bring us that, then fine, but we didn't know what else oil could—or would—do.' We are sitting in the formal reception room, *majlis*, at her son's house in Abu Dhabi. Around us are exquisite tapestries, gilt furniture, silk carpets from Iran, and display cases filled with ornate and delicate perfume bottles collected on travels throughout the Middle East. The enormous room could seat thirty people comfortably. Umm Hamad and I sit close together on one couch. We were the only ones in the room. 'Water was life in those days and we never had enough of it! You know, we used to share the sugar juice from tinned fruit cocktail straight out of the tin, it was such a luxury.' I had heard that before from one of the missionary nurses who worked in Al Ain in the 1960s. Docturah Latiefa arrived in Al Ain in 1962 as Gertrude Dyck, but was quickly renamed by the people whom she served in the hospital to honor her kindness and because it was a struggle to say her English name. Gertrude remembers social *faux pas* that occurred when a visitor to Al Ain mistook the bowl of fruit cocktail juice that was being handed around as a finger bowl and promptly dipped in her fingers. Everyone was aghast, remembers Gertrude, but no one let on and the person sitting next to the visitor calmly reached down, picked up the bowl of juice and had a little sip before passing it on.

'The water holes we scratched in the sand here were good for a day,' Umm Hamad continues. 'It was hard work in the winter, and in the summer, when people needed more water, it was killing. And the water, it was bad, so bad-tasting that only people as thirsty as we were could force it down.' Sheikh Shakhbut bin Sultan al Nahayan wanted water too; in fact he wanted water first and foremost. It was the dire necessity of finding new and reliable sources of water that convinced him, begrudgingly, to allow geologists and surveyors to look for oil in the emirate, but they had to promise to look for water first. That caveat was promptly ignored. As one of my students discovered as she researched Abu Dhabi's history, Shakhbut also permitted a pair of water dowsers to run about Abu Dhabi Island, much to the chagrin of the British agent. The dowsers promised much and soon claimed to find water just about everywhere they stepped (Al Rumaithi 2008). Looking back, they were a comic failure, but at the time it was far from funny—water was needed desperately.

Sheikh Shakhbut, depending on which source one consults, was a thorn in Britain's side, a recalcitrant miser, a xenophobe, a consummate politician, a bumbling fool or a desert savant fascinated by space exploration and BBC News on the shortwave radio. Sadly, he is portrayed most often as a miser.

One of the first Shakhbut stories I heard was that he hoarded money under his bed in the ruler's fort, Qasr al Hosn. Interestingly, this was recounted as evidence of his distrust of modern institutions like banks, but there were no banks in Abu Dhabi to distrust at that time. Sheikha Maryam, his widow, emphatically denies the story and points out that she, of all people, would know what was and was not under the bed.

Shakhbut is a fascinating figure in Abu Dhabi's history, whose reign has been totally eclipsed by the breathtaking development and convulsive change that followed his abdication. Shakhbut's caution and, it must be said, his frank distrust of the British are entirely understandable in the context of the time. The economy of Abu Dhabi had crashed when the double-whammy of cultured pearls and the Great Depression largely obliterated the market for Gulf pearls. Shakhbut had witnessed decades of British demands that alternated between 'carrots and sticks,' and mostly sticks in the form of fines and penalties. So when the British made lofty promises about oil concessions and revenues, Shakhbut was wary. Lienhardt, an anthropologist, came to Abu Dhabi in 1953, and in addition to his research was engaged as a secretary to Sheikh Shakhbut to advise him on future development. They clashed immediately and frequently for three months and then Shakhbut fired Lienhardt. Lienhardt's task was to help modernize administration, but he discovered quickly that Shakhbut was suspicious of anything that would devolve power from his hands and so the experiment was a failure. It is from Lienhardt's time that we have the story of an incident that captures the essence of Shakhbut's reticence to jump blindly and wholeheartedly into a future that the long distrusted British—now corporate oil working hand-in-hand with the Foreign Office— held out to him. The story recounts the visit of two Kuwaitis who, when they appeared in Western clothes before Shakhbut, so horrified him that his resistance to development and change hardened to granite. This story of the Kuwaitis—whose government was helping to set up schools at the time—is still told frequently but now it has a different, almost prophetic tone as if Shakhbut had been right to worry that adopting Western-style clothes was the first step on a very slippery slope.

Lienhardt's description of Abu Dhabi in 1953 gives us a feeling for the bleakness of the place. Tiny cups of foul-tasting water were sold in the one or two tea shops that managed still to eke out a living in the town. All but one of the *suqs* had been abandoned, and, as Maryam remembered, the beach in front of the Qasr al Hosn fort was the town's only latrine and dump for garbage. He also notes that the people of Abu Dhabi were increasingly upset that they were not realizing anything from the monies coming from oil exploration (Lienhardt 2001).

When the Hillyards arrived in 1953, the spot chosen to build their house was purposely far enough up the beach to the east to be sufficiently upwind of the stench of ordure and rotting carcasses that languished in the heat until the tide cleaned the area again. Tim Hillyard, his wife Susan and their young daughter Deborah were the first Europeans to live in Abu Dhabi. Hillyard worked for British Petroleum. Susan Hillyard's account of their time, difficult and challenging on better days, is a wonderful and sympathetic look into the past. She and Deborah were frequent guests at Qasr al Hosn, the ruler's palace, and so came to know the women of the ruling family at a time when they had never met a European (Hillyard 2002).

Few Emiratis other than high-ranking men in the ruling family laid eyes on anyone representing Britain or British interests. A tenet of Britain's Gulf policy was that they would not 'interfere in local matters.' They did intervene and interfered frequently in political matters, such as succession to rule and in matters that had economic repercussions, but their interaction was confined to the rulers, ruling family members and sometimes family factions in opposition to the current ruler. There was no actual British presence on land until 1939; up to that point the British ruled from Bushire and later Bahrain with non-native agents representing their interests in the towns. The appearance of strange men in the desert interior was quite a surprise, so much so that some of the first geologists and surveyors were shot at and generally harassed. Sheikh Zayed, then the governor of Al Ain town, took charge and personally escorted the exploration parties as they roamed through the surrounding desert.

It was Sheikh Zayed bin Sultan al Nahayan who replaced his older brother as ruler of Abu Dhabi in 1966. Sheikh Zayed wanted change and he wanted development and he immediately set about both. Abu Dhabi's stagnation and isolation were to end quickly. When oil was discovered offshore in 1968, Abu Dhabi exploded with a great burst of planning, design and construction that laid the basic infrastructure of roads and telecommunications, desalination plants, electricity and sewage. Hospitals and schools were built, banks and shops opened and, importantly, *buyut al shaab* (houses for the people) were erected that for most signaled the first time they had slept in a concrete structure. Abu Dhabi and its people were suddenly wrenched free from a long generation of poverty and catapulted into a complex strange world for which both the city and the people were little prepared.

Forty years later Abu Dhabi is one of the wealthiest cities in the world; the memory of poverty has been largely erased and is rarely discussed by the younger generation of Emiratis. Oil revenues have transformed the cultural landscape of Abu Dhabi and, indeed, the UAE, although until recently it was the media darling Dubai that received most of the attention. Now it is Abu Dhabi that is making headlines with ambitious and glamorous projects such as Masdar, a zero-carbon emission city, an entire island devoted to Formula 1 racing, and of course Saadiyat Island. The city is home—at the moment—to over a million people, most of whom are transnational workers. The beach that was the latrine has been covered by tons of compacted rock and sand, paved and landscaped in order to expand the road that runs along the top of the island.

Oil, the reward for the pious?

A fascinating topic for discussion has been to ask Emiratis how they perceive the presence of great reserves of oil under the pretty much inhospitable land, and what would happen if the oil disappeared. One cool January evening in 2003 I sat with three women on the sand at Ladies Beach, a gender-segregated swimming beach in Abu Dhabi, and we talked about what oil meant to them. '*Walah*, you know I believe that oil has been a reward from Allah to us.[2] We had so very little for so long; really even the good times were hardly excellent because of the climate and the desert. So I think that oil was a treasure hidden away for us.' Sara is in her early forties and is normally busy with her children's hectic schedule of private English lessons and tutoring in math so it is unusual for her to be with us for our evening walks. Alanood, sitting next to Sara, leans forward and chuckles before she speaks. 'You know, I sort of believe that too but then I also know that it has as much to do with dinosaurs and organic matter that were here before us.' She pauses for a moment and thinks. 'I suppose it can be both, after all; it is Allah who decides where everything occurs and where it dies.'

The third member of our group, Alyazya, paces around us in the sand because, she says, she burns more calories than if she just sat. Alyazya is a thoughtful young woman in her early thirties and speaks eloquently so I am eager to hear her views on the matter. She is very thoughtful tonight and makes us wait several more minutes. In the meantime, Alanood speaks up again. 'The whole evolution thing is so confusing for anyone who believes in God; how are we supposed to reconcile what science tells us with what the Quran says?' This is a question that I consistently skirt in classes because I am often uncomfortable with my own views on the issue and I tell my friends that. 'But there is that intelligent design theory too; doesn't that bring the two closer together?' Alanood confides that she has been searching the internet for information about creationism and intelligent design and struggling to understand how a Muslim woman should make sense of it all. 'I sometimes wonder if we can make sense of it all,' says Alyazya as she walks behind us. 'Sometimes I want to think that Allah has given us the information that we need to know and that there are some things, like dinosaurs and the evolution of the species, that he has withheld information about and so we struggle to make sense of what science tells us. There is nothing in the Quran that says we should not use knowledge or science and yet we worry when the two seem to be at odds. What we know from revelation is what we need to live properly and righteously as believers, and perhaps what we learn from science is that we are expected to use our brains to figure out the rest of the story.'

'But to get back to Jane's question about oil, I think that most Emiratis think that our oil, and we do think of it as "ours," is a reward from Allah.'

Alyazya went on to say that it was not only Emiratis but the Arabs of the peninsula who thought this way. 'Our first blessing was the Prophet Muhammad and the glorious Quran. The second blessing, oil, came hundreds of years later when the Islamic empires had dissolved; we were under the control of European powers like the British and the French and had become disparate tribal groups fighting over water. Oil gave us wealth and it gave us power again and to a degree it earned us some respect.' We went on to discuss whether blessings are earned or whether they are bestowed by God in what Christians would call grace. These women thought both were true, but in the case of oil it seemed to them to be more of a reward, a blessing bestowed on a people who had earned it. 'Earned how?' I asked. 'Through the belief and piety of our ancestors.' For Alyazya this meant that it was the steadfast belief and righteous living of generations which had been rewarded by God.

This I was to hear many more times when discussing oil and what it represented to Emiratis. Four years after the beach discussion I talked with a group of women who worked together at a government agency over coffee in one of the offices. On this occasion I asked how contemporary Emiratis measured up to their ancestors in terms of steadfast belief and righteous living; in other words, was the blessing earned by their forefathers being honored or squandered? I think that I heard gasps as I asked the question and it was followed by a protracted silence. 'Do you mean have we become people not deserving of the blessing?' I said no, that wasn't exactly my question. I put it another way. 'If Emiratis believe that the oil was placed here by Allah as a blessing that was a reward for the people's strong and steadfast belief and their righteous lives, as many do believe, then the next logical question is to ask whether you think that you are now living lives that are equally steadfast in belief.'

'I think that is the same thing, really,' Hanouf answers with a smile. 'Many might say that we are not living the way we should now, that we have become too wealthy, too arrogant and too self-absorbed and so we have lost the level of piety and dedication that our grandparents had. But is that even possible in our modern world? I wonder.' Two of the other women agree with Hanouf and say that such dedication was possible because there were not the distractions in the old days. 'They had no TV, no schools and homework, no movies, no malls; they had family and they had

Allah. We have such busy lives with work, children, husbands, shopping and everything else that it is difficult to think of Allah all the time.' I comment that I see stickers on many cars that remind people 'not to forget to think of Allah.' 'Yes, exactly. We need reminders now in this new age.'

Asmaa has been silent up until now and she returns us to the question of honoring or squandering the blessing. 'I think we are squandering it, honestly. We are spoiled, we live privileged lives with maids and cooks and we spend money on ourselves when so many people on this earth live in poverty.' Her co-workers disagree. 'We have to live! We give *zakat* to charities and needy people, we are generous and we are fair but we live in a different age than our ancestors! Think of the money that the country gives in relief aid, in development aid to Africa and other countries; we are conscious of our blessing and share it with others.' Asmaa is not convinced and reminds them of the labor camps on the outskirts of all Emirati cities. 'What about those people? We bring them here to work for us and build our country yet we keep them in places not fit for animals. How is that righteous? How is that fair? It is neither and such behavior does us all harm, I am sure of it.'

There are two issues that weigh uncomfortably and so are discussed fairly often. The first is the lifestyles that Emiratis are able to enjoy now; and the second is the responsibilities that come with wealth. They are interrelated of course, but most Emiratis prefer to discuss them as separate issues. In class discussions I am frequently asked if I think there is a double standard applied to the wealthy Arabs of the Gulf. 'Do people talk about what Bill Gates spends on his cars? No, they don't. They talk about his foundation that gives things away but they don't criticize him for what he drives.' True, I say. So, the discussion continues with questions about why Gulf Arabs should be singled out for criticism and soon turns to the fact that oil just happened, no one had to work for it other than to get it out of the ground. 'Does that make it less ours? No, some countries have other natural resources like abundant water, rubber, wood and fertile land and no one claims that they don't deserve what they have or that they shouldn't enjoy the profits they gain from it! So why not the same measuring stick for us and oil?' Good question.

I am sitting with a friend, Mouza, and her cousins in the family living room at Mouza's house and we are trying to carry on an adult conversation despite the presence of five rambunctious children. In between quelling disputes over the television remote control and separating sparring boys, we talk about the responsibility of wealth. I know Mouza well enough to be aware of her constant charity that takes many forms. She gives regular and hefty donations to the Red Crescent, contributes to children's relief in Palestine, supports schools and mosques in other Arab countries and feeds several hundred each night during Ramadan. Her cousins, I assume, are much like her. They are, but even more so.

'How could we possibly live if we didn't share what we have with others? I couldn't sleep and I wouldn't want to anyway.' Hamda pulls one of her children close to her on the couch. 'What sort of parents would we be if we didn't worry about all children, everywhere?' Her cousins all nod in unison. '*Sahih*,' they say, meaning right or correct. Each of them then mentions a few charities that they give to, appeals to which they have responded, organizations that they support and those that their husbands give to separately. 'We give doubly in most cases,' says Fatima. 'Because I give from my money and then I tell my husband that he should give as well.' Emirati women have complete control of their own money and it is the husband's duty to carry all household and family expenses. 'Me too, but usually it is the other way around, my husband comes home and tells me that he has heard about a great need somewhere.'

'We don't talk about this much in public, you know, because you are to give silently, anonymously in Islam,' says Hamda. 'It isn't really giving from the heart if you need to be acknowledged, recognized and awarded for your action. Allah will reward you in time.' I mention to the women that someone told me once that if the private contributions of Emiratis given just to Red Crescent were added up that it would be a staggering annual sum. One government official had also told me that the amount of money donated to charities by Sheikha Fatima, the widow of Sheikh Zayed bin Sultan and the mother of the Crown Prince of Abu Dhabi, Sheikh Mohammad bin Zayed (and others who hold ministerial positions), was equal to that given by some countries, but because it was personal money it was not considered a part of the UAE's charitable giving. My friends were very proud to hear that. 'That is as it should be; Sheikha Fatima is right and proper and we should all follow her example.'

4

OUR NEW LIVES BEHIND WALLS

Daily life became much easier in Abu Dhabi when the basics of life such as drinking water were readily available. The first houses built for people were not a great success because the concrete held heat and people were unable to sleep. That problem was solved as electricity lines extended across the town and air conditioning was introduced. Those early houses did not last long and none survive intact. They were abandoned as new, bigger houses were built further inland, away from the Fort and the beach where few people had lived before. As Emiratis left for their new houses, the old ones were rented out to the increasing numbers of foreign workers who arrived to work in construction and other jobs that the growing city offered.

'That's when we moved away from the heart of the city. We live in what you Americans call suburbs now.' Fakhera winks at me because she is pleased that I seem impressed by her use of the word suburb. She and I are sitting in the garden of her house which is, as she says, in the suburbs. It is in an area called al Mushref, southwest of the old town. The streets in al Mushref are wide, the houses are large and the walls are high. High though they may be, the walls do not keep out the sounds of construction nearby. Fakhera is not happy that her neighbors are adding on to their house and she scowls every time she hears a loud noise. 'I don't know why they have to make it bigger again,' she mutters. 'They did this a couple of years ago too.' I suggest that perhaps a son has married and they need more space for the new couple to have private quarters. 'No, no, the boys are all married long since. I don't know what this is for.' Fakhera is concerned that the new extension of the neighbor's house will be higher than her walls. 'What if that happens? Then they will be able to look down into my garden and maybe even into the house! I will have no privacy.' From previous visits I know that Fakhera is frequently concerned about her neighbors. I ask if she has gone to visit them in order to see the plans for the extension of the house. 'No, I can't just go and visit them like that, I don't know them, and they aren't Manasir, so how would I go there?' Fakhera is a widow who, rather surprisingly, refuses to go live with her son, Khalid, who lives in Al Ain. Fakhera has her youngest daughter, Aisha, at home so she is not alone, but it is unusual to have no male relative in the house. 'It is so strange to live next to people that we don't know; that never happened in the past,' says Fakhera. '*Abadan*: we lived in communities. Now we live in the suburbs.'

Life is very different now, say many women, because they have less freedom and less independence than women had in the days before oil. Yes, they agree, they have lots of money and material things that are wonderful and have made life much easier. What they don't have any more is the ability to walk to their sister's house or to their mother's house in the early morning. What they don't have now is a community life, a sense of living together. Abu Dhabi has grown into a big, modern city with fancy hotels, malls, cinemas, coffee shops and restaurants, but, say the women, it is men who have the freedom of movement to access these new conveniences and attractions, not them. The new Abu Dhabi represents luxury and easy lives for many Emirati women, but some note that women have lost the freedom to act independently as, they tell me, women did in the days before oil.

Alyazia and her children escape to Al Ain whenever possible because she says life is normal there. She was born in Al Ain and considers it home even though she has lived in Abu Dhabi for over twenty years. 'I don't feel like I belong in Abu Dhabi. I don't think that anyone feels like they belong there.' Alyazia's husband is so busy with work that he rarely takes a day off, and so she and the children have the driver take them to Al Ain every Thursday afternoon and they stay for the weekend. 'It's only in Al Ain that I feel normal and I want my children to know Al Ain, to know the feeling of community.' Alyazia's comment is not unusual and, in fact, Al Ain is often touted as the 'most Emirati city' because so many Emiratis live there and it has so far been spared the sorts of megadevelopments that have transformed Abu Dhabi and Dubai. For me it was the location of the national museum, significant archaeological sites and the place to escape at least some of the summer humidity. I had taken busloads of students to Al Ain and thought I knew it quite well. I did know one Al Ain well but I had not been introduced to the other, the Emirati one, until Alyazia included me on one of the weekend retreats to the family compound. Then I began to understand what she was missing.

In the quiet back streets of Al Ain are neighborhoods that still bear the names of the original oasis around which people lived in the past. There are date palms everywhere and the shade is deep and wonderfully cool on hot days. Alyazia tells me how important the date palm was to people before the arrival of all the changes that oil money brought. 'Yes, of course for the dates, but for so much more. There was not one part of the palm tree that wasn't used. The wood of the trunk was the only wood we had so it was made into planks for building, poles for tents, used for boat frames and lots of other things. We fed the date nut to the goats. The fronds were stripped down, dried in the sun and sometimes dyed in different colors. Then the dried fronds were woven into baskets and mats. The rib down the center of the larger fronds was used to make lightweight tables, crates and boxes for storage.' We are standing in the midst of towering date palms as Alyazia talks, and she is having fun demonstrating techniques with the handy props that lie at our feet. 'But still, it was just what came from the palm. Look at the shade here that we are enjoying, this is important shade!' She points across an irrigation channel. 'Look there, vegetables growing in the shade. In the shade cast by the tall palms people were able to plant vegetables that would have never survived in the strong sun here.' Alyazia is right, the palm allowed for the development of what is called an oasis economy. In the UAE an important part of the oasis economy was the *falaj* system of irrigation that moved water through small hard-packed mud canals and channels so that more palm gardens could be planted.

Most contemporary house compounds have date palms too, and for the long-established families of Al Ain the palms at home are in addition to those they own in the irrigated, oasis areas that have been growing palms and producing dates for hundreds of years. Dates are still a staple food. They are served to each and every guest with *gahwa*, the coffee that welcomes visitors no matter what their arrival time. Dates are eaten fresh in late summer and early autumn when the harvest is underway. Date palms planted on median dividers, in city gardens and as public landscaping are fair game to anyone who wants to exert the effort to pick them. Cars pull over, as often as not still half blocking the lane, and people jump out armed with hooked sticks and baskets or cloths and gather the ripe dates that are within their reach. The government has devoted a considerable amount of resources and attention to increase the country's date production, and the results are impressive. The country now counts 40 million date palm trees, with 33 million in Abu Dhabi Emirate. There are 110 varieties of dates grown in the UAE and over 500,000 metric tons are harvested annually. Once a date importer, now the UAE is a major exporter.

Al Ain has a rural atmosphere and it is common for families to keep chickens, milk cows, goats and even camels at the back of the compound. Sheikha Hussa, the President's mother, is famous for her farm products and some Al Ain women will eat nothing but the yoghurt, eggs and chickens from the Sheikha's farm. Other women are rightfully proud of their own homegrown products, and though they may not know very many words in English, when they discuss the relative merits of eggs and chickens, their Emirati dialect is peppered with 'organic' and 'all natural', both spoken with a slightly self-conscious pronunciation. I would like to see some of these lady farmers competing at a country fair; there would be stiff competition. It is not the competition that motivates them though; it is, I am told, the self-reliance of the old days. 'If you wanted to eat it, you had to have it in your flock, so if you were a hard worker and took care, you had chickens, goats and maybe even a cow besides the camels.' Grandma made sure that I had been given the tour of her farm area that was tucked away at the back of the property on my first visit to the family compound. She is extraordinarily proud of her organically fed, free-range chickens and eggs. It was the taste of her chickens that prompted a lunchtime discussion because one of her grandchildren refused to eat. 'They taste funny. I only like the chicken that comes from the shop in Abu Dhabi.' If the grandchild had been nine or ten years old I would have chalked up her comment as something kids just do; like I refused to eat green beans at home but would gladly have them at my aunt's house. This grandchild was almost twenty-two years old and there was a little more at issue. 'Why does she even have chickens any more?' she demanded. 'It's not like she needs them; why doesn't she just buy them like everyone else does?' I reminded her that Grandma also took great pride in her dates, *harees*, coffee and everything else that came out of the kitchen and, in fact, was known to transport great quantities of her home products to London for the summer (apparently unbeknownst to the officials at Heathrow). 'But why don't we ask your Grandma?' It took us some time to find Grandma in the compound; she rarely ate a full lunch with us and so had left the dining room.

It was more of an argument than a conversation that we started with Grandma, because she seized the opportunity to lecture her granddaughter on what she perceived to be her shortcomings and then on all the things that were wrong in Emirati life today. 'You can't cook! You cannot cook even the simplest foods! Your mother cannot cook! What would you do without those idiot cooks at your house? You would starve. How can you not know how to do the things that a woman has always done? I just don't understand what will become of you.' Maitha was stunned and immediately defensive. 'But I don't need to know those things; we have the maids and the cooks to do that sort of work, why should I have to know? And if you are angry that my mother doesn't know, whose fault is that? Who should have taught her?' Grandma ignored the bait and continued on. 'All Emiratis have someone else doing the work for them! How can you all have become so lazy? You are spoiled,

spoiled people who cannot even wash your own clothes. What will become of you when the money runs out? What then?'

There was no real end to the argument; grandmother and granddaughter share a certain strain of stubbornness. Vexed, granddaughter stomped off across the compound and Grandma muttered under her *burqah*. Do you really worry, I asked? 'Yes, yes I do worry,' she said. 'I look at the way they live and I worry all the time. It isn't natural to turn your lives over to servants! Mothers don't spend time with their children; they hire nannies and maids for that now and so we have children who spend more time with a foreign woman than their own mothers!' She harrumphed in disgust. 'They complain about losing their identity! I laugh at that! They haven't lost it, they gave it away a long time ago when they filled their houses with servants and the streets with foreigners to build this big fancy country!' We sat down on the chairs near the cow shed. 'It isn't true that my daughter can't cook, you know.' I said that I did know that was true. 'I don't worry about my daughter's generation so much as I do those who are younger. My daughter remembers the old ways. She used to go out with her father to tend the camels in the desert when she was young, you know. She loved it and since she was the eldest child, and the only child for a long while, her father loved taking her with him. She learned to respect nature and hard work on those trips and when she was home, here with me, she also learned to respect hard work and all that it takes to run a family.' Grandma was quiet for a bit. 'The generation born after all the changes, after the money and the building, that is the generation that has lost its way and the will to do anything other than show off with fancy clothes and cars. What will they do if this all disappears? What will they do? They have become soft and lazy and that means weak; we were never weak in the old days.'

Many women of Grandma's generation, born in the late 1930s and '40s, express the same worries about what the future holds for their grandchildren. Interestingly, all those I have spoken to use the same words: weak, soft and lazy. On the other hand, even in their seventies, all the women are convinced that they could go back to the old days quite easily, if not comfortably. They are sadly confident that their grandchildren, and even in some cases their own children, could not. Grandma stands up and walks over to check on her cows in their air-conditioned stall. I suggest that perhaps even she has gotten a little spoiled and if not she, then certainly the cows. She smiles and laughs. 'Yes, I suppose we all have, but the difference is that I know what is involved; the youth of this country have no idea.' I point out that only something as dreadful as a nuclear disaster would force young Emiratis to live without electricity and running water again. Her response is to remind me that the wealth came overnight and it can leave overnight. This too is a frequent comment and not from older women only; women in their forties remark also that everything they have can go as easily as it has come.

My presence in the Al Ain neighborhoods draws attention; foreigners are not common in some of the areas. Even when I am just driving through on my way to a friend's house, I am noticed and scrutinized carefully by the children playing in the streets and drivers passing me. The homes in these areas are surrounded by high walls, so often an entire street runs down between two massive walls that are broken only by rather narrow gated entries. The families here have lived in the vicinity for generations and so they have built new, modern houses and compounds on land that their grandfathers tended 100 years ago. The family connections between the compounds are close and intricate, with grandparents, sons, daughters, cousins and grandchildren split up along roughly paternal and maternal lines on one side of the street or the other. One family that I know well lives in homes on both sides of the entire road. On the one side is the eldest surviving son who is now a grandfather many times over. He has built houses for each of his sons on the compound as they married. His sister, who married a cousin who, by virtue of being in the same patrilineage, had access to family land in the area, lives across the street with her husband and their sons and visiting married daughters. In the normal course of events the children of the brother and sister would have married according to the preferred *bint 'amm* way (daughter of paternal uncle) and so those grandchildren have maternal grandmother and paternal grandfather within yelling distance. One large family at whose homes I spend time has brother, uncle, father-in-law and grandfather on one side of the lane, where they too have a house, and on the other side, about 500 meters away, are sister, mother, aunt, mother-in-law and grandmother. Grandchildren roam back and forth between the two compounds and the route is littered with abandoned bicycles and toys.

The women of the associated houses traverse the lane throughout the day and night. Sometimes they are bringing food from their kitchen or looking for missing children (or toys) but mostly just to visit and talk. They talk about their children, schools, the pros and cons of getting a tutor, dentists and braces, footballs, WiFi games, upcoming weddings, and the next trip to the tailor for new dresses: the everyday details of lives. WiFi set-ups bought for the children are now popular with their mothers, and one friend complained that she had developed tennis elbow playing against her son. The black *'abayah* that covers them in the city is discarded here in the privacy of the family neighborhood that includes the streets that run between the separate compounds, and only a *shaylah*, a head-scarf, is worn. The *jalabba* (long house dresses) they wear are brightly colored and the *kandoura* are decorated with embroidery around the neckline, the cuffs and sometimes around the hem.

One day, sitting with five women on the verandah at a friend's house, I remarked that Al Ain always seemed more relaxed to me and that everyone was much more casual than when we were in Abu Dhabi. *'Akeed,'* (of course) was the quick response from the women around me, 'because here we still have freedom.' When I pointed out that all of them were constantly on the go in Abu Dhabi and all had, except one, spacious villas with manicured gardens in the capital, I was told that it was qualitatively different. 'We can't walk out of our house and cross the street to visit each other in Abu Dhabi!' Their amused expressions told me that I was missing the point. Alyazia, my patient friend, tried to explain. 'Here the walls are put up to keep the children safe, to prevent the goats and chickens from wandering off and to protect the house and garden from blowing sands. In Abu Dhabi the walls are like prison walls—meant to keep us in and everybody else out.' But surely, I argued, that is just in the eye of the beholder. No, they all agreed that it was different. 'In Abu Dhabi the walls created little fortresses against cars, foreigners [here with an apologetic nod to me] and the non-related Emiratis who live around us. There we have houses that must be protected from our Emirati neighbors and their eyes as much as the prying, inquisitive eyes of foreigners.'

'But the only foreigners around your houses are the ones who work for you,' I countered. 'And I have gone walking with all of you at night so I know you can walk out of the compound!' Again, the women replied that walking for exercise was different; it was not the same thing as being able to visit your sister. I agreed with that but then suggested that perhaps it was just the spread-out nature of the neighborhoods in Abu Dhabi that made walking to a relative's house difficult. 'Well yes, that is part of it of course; we are all separated by roads and buildings. Abu Dhabi has become a big city. But what we mean is that once we leave our gate we are in the public view, we are on a street where everyone can see us.' Mimi, who is Alyazia's youngest sister, laughed. 'Why did you think we always walk at night? No one can see us in the dark!'

I had heard this expressed before by several other women who chafed against the restrictions placed on their movements. Oshah, in her fifties when we met, referred to Abu Dhabi as 'fortress Abu Dhabi' because she always felt as if she was in prison in the city and her every move noted. '*Ya Rabi*, God help you if you just poke your head through the gate to look down your street in Abu Dhabi! If you are not wearing the perfect '*abayah* and a matching *shaylah*, if your feet are not in some instantly recognizable designer sandal and you haven't perfumed yourself, you will hear soon enough that something is wrong in your house!' Had this happened, I asked? 'Not to me,' she replied, 'I am too smart for that!' Oshah smiled a little ruefully. 'It happened to one of my nieces who was just walk-ing in the garden and thought she might walk down the street a bit for more exercise. Someone passing in a car must have seen her standing in the entry to the compound and the next thing we know there is a rumor that she is having an affair because she was "look-ing for someone"—that was the only believable explanation for her to be there!' Oshah was still incredulous, but she went on to add a little gossip of her own. 'It isn't as if my niece is like that woman in

Bateen [an area of Abu Dhabi] who was sneaking her boyfriend into the house after her husband left for the day.'

Freedom of movement became a topic for class discussion soon after my conversation with Oshah when we were planning a fieldtrip to Sharjah to visit its historic district and museums. Several students said that they would not be allowed to go on the fieldtrip. I protested and reminded them that all parents had signed an agreement whereby they gave their permission for their daughter to participate in all activities that were required for class, including fieldtrips. In fact, I argued (I love fieldtrips) they really didn't have to ask their parents again since permission had, legally, already been given. After a chorus of gasps there was total silence as twenty-three students stared at me. Finally one spoke out. 'Are you crazy, Miss? Do you know what would happen if my father discovered that I had been on a fieldtrip, off the island, in Sharjah without his permission?' The class erupted into a loud and heated discussion. 'If it weren't off the island, then maybe I could go.' 'I can't go on any trips ever; what if someone was to see me and then word would go round that I was out—that would be enough to ruin my name!'

I certainly understand parents' concerns about fieldtrips out of the city. Parents might have several objections, such as the appalling number of accidents on the roads that involve buses and the possibility of their daughter being left behind somewhere by accident. I also knew from experience that students sometimes used their parents as an excuse when they didn't want to do something or when they weren't particularly interested in a trip. Some students were simply not allowed to leave the campus for any reason and others were also prohibited from attending lectures and concerts held during the evening. In most cases the restrictions placed on the student are more numerous if she is from the ruling family, but that is not always true. In only a few cases do the restrictions seem connected to conservatism—religious or otherwise. Students who wear the *niqab*, the full black cloth face-veil, on campus where it is interpreted as religious conservatism are, in my experience, the first on the bus for a fieldtrip.

Rather unexpectedly, the number of students who say they cannot go on fieldtrips has risen in the last three years. It is common for me to have the same student in several different courses as she progresses through the program and so it was quite surprising to be told by students I knew that they 'cannot go on any fieldtrips.' 'And when did that start?' is my usual response. 'Oh, it's my father, Miss; he has decided that I shouldn't be seen doing those sorts of things.' I never do get a full explanation of what sorts of things we are talking about. 'That's just the new status marker! Act like a *sheikha* and people will think you are from a really powerful family!' Salma and her friends are hanging out in the classroom after class. 'But that can't work, surely. Everyone knows who is a *sheikha* and who is not,' I protested. 'Exactly, that's how stupid it is but more and more are doing it.'

'What,' I asked, 'does one compete over when so many families have so much money?' 'They compete on this sort of thing. Who can't go because they are so special? Who has to have security at a wedding? Who has British women for chaperones? It's all that stuff and it is just dumb,' says Salma who is clearly not impressed with this new development. 'Yes, I am angry about it because it is so contrary to education, to women working and what the government talks about. It is going backwards.'

I find it particularly interesting to listen to the different understandings of phrases such as freedom of movement, independent decision-making, autonomy and independence. Freedom of movement for most of the students is independent decision-making; that they can make a decision to go to a place or event and act on their decision without interference or indeed consultation. I press the issue. 'But is this freedom of movement?' 'So what if someone sees you? Who would talk? Who would start a rumor? Who is going to recognize you in Sharjah?' I ask these questions looking at twenty plus students who are, on a normal class day, dressed in jeans and pretty tight t-shirts under their *'abayahs*. Two-thirds of them are wearing a considerable amount of make-up and have on their feet high-heeled shoes that in my conservative American mind look a lot more like something worn on a hot date than to a university class. 'What's the issue here?' I ask again.

There are lots of answers. 'Mostly, I think it is distant family members that we worry about. Someone who doesn't really know us but might recognize us and then say later that she saw *fulan bint fulan* (so and so's daughter) out without a brother.' The rest of the class agrees with this partially but there is no consensus. Some parents are stricter than others, some are very cautious and protective and some are not. Parental concerns may arise because of status, or rather the perception of status, or just the safety and wellbeing of their daughter. In every class discussion there has been a full spectrum of positions.

The next reading assigned was a classic that I had read as an undergraduate, on the politics of public and private in Arab society (Nelson 1973). For the next several class sessions we argued the constructed boundaries that mark public space/public behavior and private space/private behavior and how those are negotiated and sometimes enforced. Nelson's argument is that the separation of the genders in the Arab world had been misunderstood and over-emphasized by the primarily male researchers who had no access to what they called 'the private sphere of women' (Nelson 1973:551). The students were fascinated with Nelson's article, and even more when I told them that she had been my teacher in Cairo when I was a student. Most students have more than a cursory understanding of Said's Orientalism and quickly noted that Nelson's argument pre-dated his critique (Said 1979).

We had been discussing how Western men have perceived Arab women in another context. In 1903 a German traveler named Burchardt came to Abu Dhabi and was the guest of Sheikh Zayed the Great, who ruled from 1885 to 1909. Burchardt's account and photographs of his time include the fact that Sheikh Zayed's wife cooked his meal for him (Burchardt 2009). He mentions that she inquired if he liked the food, because apparently he hadn't eaten everything that had been given to him. She is not named in his account and Burchardt never sees her. Even so, Burchardt's reference to a woman is rare. When the students were then reading Nelson's article, they immediately seized onto the reference made to the powerful political role that the women of the ruling families had here in the earlier days. 'In the old days women had much more power than they do now!' 'You should come and talk to my grandmother about this; she will tell you how different it is now.'

I met with many grandmothers and mothers to pursue this topic, and in fact the theme of public/private and freedom/restriction has spilled into other classes and into other semesters. When women of all generations talk about these concepts, there is always an economic factor; women had (have and will have) freedom of movement in and out of public places because we were economic actors. 'We used to hold the purse, you know.' Khalood, or Mama Khalood as she is called by all in deference to her age and wisdom, lived her younger years in Al Ain and now lives with her second son in Abu Dhabi. 'The men were gone from us for pearling when the dates became ripe and so we took care of the date harvest every year.' The pre-oil day's economic cycle included the fishing season, the pearling season and the date harvest. The summer pearling season, in which the boats started from Abu Dhabi town and used Dalma Island as their base for the duration, ran for about three months starting in early June (Heard-Bey 1982:185). During the pearling season, men traveled up from the oasis settlements to participate and that meant leaving the women behind to deal with the date harvest. The harvest was hard work and the women did have some help from related men who had stayed behind either because of health, age or other responsibilities or, as in one man's case, an abhorrence of the sea. Some families relied on help from their *badu* (Bedouin) extended family that would camp near the palm groves and cool shade during the hot months of the summer. Dates were eaten fresh, boiled and preserved in a variety of ways for use over the coming year. A substantial portion was eaten fresh as the harvest progressed (Heard-Bey 1982:177). Dates were also bartered, traded and sold. 'We used to give a portion of the crop to our *badu* relatives who helped. They got to eat lots of fresh dates as we harvested and all of the women worked together to sort, dry and boil the rest. They needed dates to survive when they went out (of the oasis) again.' Maryam's family was '*hadr da'iman*,' always settled in the oasis, at least as far back as she knows. 'But we were not at all cut off from the tribe who still moved their camels through the desert. We exchanged goats and vegetables for camels, and in the summer when they were here we used to help with the weaving and sewing of new tents.' The communities of the coast, the mountains, the oases and the desert were linked not only by tribal affiliation, kinship and marriage but also symbiotically; no one community could really survive without the other (Hawker 2008; Heard-Bey 1982). The disjuncture between nomadic and settled life has often been characterized as abrupt, irreversible and, for those who settle, sure to dissipate their honesty, morals, worth and 'asabiyaa, the tribal code that binds, protects and, in the minds of some, makes the Bedouin infinitely more honorable than their town cousins (Khaldun 1958). While this is the sort of perspective that has encouraged us to engage in nostalgia for a romanticized image of 'the primitive' that has been appropriated by the tourist industry in the UAE, it does not represent reality now or in the past here in the UAE.

Many older Emiratis do talk about the hard work involved in pearling and fishing, but I have not had frequent opportunities to be able to talk to older men. Luckily, a group of students interviewed Khames al Romaithi who tells animated stories about how rough life was on the pearling boats. One such story recounts how an accident damaged the boat and it seemed as if they would be forced to make repairs and lose a month's worth of pearls. No one could afford that, as most of the men had already borrowed against what they hoped to make that season. Al Romaithi decided that they must stay out and dive for pearls so he stayed awake every night for the next fifteen nights to bail water out of the bilge. It was suffocatingly hot below deck and very cramped. He was bruised and cut by sharp wood and crude nails and exhausted from his efforts but they were able to stay afloat. He laughed when other men asked him how he was able to keep going all night when he had also been diving during the day. 'I will never complain in front of you men! But when I get home to my mother, then I will cry out loud.' Al Romaithi was a young man then. He stayed in pearling and worked his way up to the top of the ladder and eventually became a pearl merchant of some renown.

'There was nothing easy about life in the desert! It was a hard life made up of hard days.' Muhammad, like my grandfather, remembers the hard work and hard life of the old days and says that they are good only for those people who did not live through them. His wife, Khadija, isn't quite so sure. They are both in their late seventies, well cared for by children and adored by their seventeen grandchildren. I am informed that they have both become 'scofflaws' in their old age, and perhaps that is the reason why they meet me together—rather unusual given that I don't know the family well. It is more common for women to receive me in the women's sitting room and rare that any of the men of the family would come in when a guest was present. Khadija wears a *burqah* and her *shaylah* hangs loose down her back. She nods while her husband talks and tells me about life in the old days. Muhammad tells me how strong he was in those days. 'Strong because we pulled the big nets from the sea and they were heavy with fish. And strong because we had to row when there was no wind. We were strong young men.' Grandchildren roam in and out of the room as we are talking; hearing that Grandpa is telling stories, some sit down around his feet to listen. He is known for his storytelling and poetry. He loves to tell the children scary stories such as Um Duwais, the temptress who is really an old hag; and Salama and her daughters. Salama is a *jinni*, a spirit, who resides at the bottom of the Gulf near the Hormuz Straits. When she spots a ship on the horizon she whirls around creating enormous waves and a whirlpool that will pull the ship down so that she and her daughters can devour the sailors. Fear of Salama, we are told, led sailors to carry goats on board their ships. When a whirlpool was sighted a goat or two would be thrown overboard to feed Salama in the hope that she would spare their lives. This folktale has its roots in the turbulent waters of the Strait where whirlpools are common. Supposedly there was another incident that gave the story even more credibility. A passenger ship sailing to India was overloaded with both passengers and cargo. When the ship entered the Straits of Hormuz the weather deteriorated and a great storm rose up with high seas and strong winds. The captain, so the story goes, used the story of Salama the *jinni* to frighten his passengers so that they would throw their luggage and cargo overboard. They did and the ship was lightened sufficiently to maneuver through the storm and treacherous waters.

Muhammad tells the tale of Salama, and the children scream with excitement and anticipation; they know the story well and are acting like scary *jinn* as their grandfather talks.

Today Muhammad tells only one story and the children are disappointed. He is tired, he says, because they drove to Dubai yesterday and he is not used to the hustle and bustle. I have already been told that the Dubai visit was for medical treatment and that Muhammad should rest this afternoon. The children go off to play elsewhere and Muhammad sits with us for a short while. He leaves us to 'attend to things.' Khadija sighs. Her worry is apparent. They have been married since she was fourteen years old and he was eighteen—over sixty years now and the bond between them is visible. There were no other wives, only Khadija. 'He was strong in his youth,' she says. I answer with *ma sha'allah*, which translates as it is God's will that it be so. She smiles and thinks for a moment or two. 'He dislikes the city as much as I do but for him it is different, better. He can go out when he likes and he is a man on the street so that is *'aady*, normal or acceptable. For us, for women nowadays, it has changed so much—so many strangers everywhere, strange men on all the streets—it is impossible to go out without someone you know.' Khadija is referring to the fact that Emirati women and girls are often accompanied by a male relative when they go to a public venue like a shopping mall, restaurant or cinema. Khadija's concerns echo those I have heard before but never heard clearly explained. Some women have told me that this is a new phenomenon that stems from a fear of the 'strange men now living here.' But others tell me that the custom is an old one, that a brother or uncle goes with them to protect them. 'Protect from what or whom?' 'From the idea that we might be doing something we shouldn't and protecting us from the unwanted attention of men.'

I ask Khadija if it is because leaving the house takes her into the public, onto streets that have many different people walking and driving. 'When we go outside [of the house] it is like we are entering another land—we see faces everywhere but we don't know them—they are strangers, they don't speak our language, they don't look or act like us.' 'Are you afraid?' I ask. 'No, no. It isn't fear at all, and it isn't that I don't know that these people are here to work.' She thinks for a minute or two. 'If there is fear, and maybe there is a little, it is because all those strangers are running things and so when we look we no longer see our people—we see only foreigners.' We talked about what is often called the Emirati dependency on foreign labor for some time. 'I think the men are somehow angry inside because they must feel shame about this— our men were hard workers, they were strong and they were proud and they did everything that needed doing for us to live.' Khadija giggled a bit. 'Now it seems that the hardest thing they face is not wrinkling their *kandoura* during the day!' She continued to chuckle at her joke. 'How can our young women want to marry a man who has never proven himself?' I had no answer to that.

I return to the subject of freedom of movement before Khadija gets too far into something else. 'The walls around this house here that were supposed to give us privacy have actually marked the difference between men and women now. The women are supposed to be inside the walls and if we want to go out it is a big, complicated affair because we don't go alone and so we have to have a sister, a cousin, a daughter—even one of the grandchildren. Then we have to be dressed properly, with good *kandouras*, fashionable shoes and bags. Then we have to get the driver to come. By the time we do all that I am tired and I don't want to go anywhere.'

I have experienced the 'getting ready' process at several homes and Khadija's remarks rang very true. Getting ready to go out is a complicated and elaborate process. It can be shortened considerably by donning *niqab*, the cloth veil that hangs just below the eyes and is fastened to a cap that is, at least to my eye, very nun-like. One friend who is an early riser regularly dons *niqab*, summons the driver and runs errands and goes shopping with impunity at a time when shops and malls are just opening. She is also a well-respected woman married to an equally well-respected man and both are from a very well-respected family. 'Still, even with me and you know I don't really care, but I have to look as if I do.' I know her to be very religious and tell her I have always just assumed that she wore *niqab* for modesty. 'But that isn't Islam! That's a recent addition that we borrowed from somewhere, probably Saudi. It is handy though because, truly, unless someone knows you well they can't tell who you are!' But, I ask, who are you protecting yourself from? 'Oh, just about everyone these days. If I wear that the workers won't stare—at least the Muslim ones won't! I don't care about the Western foreigners and, anyway, they tend to stare longer when I wear *niqab* than when I don't. But it isn't because of foreigners, it is for other Emiratis who may see, may recognize me and then perhaps tell someone that I was seen doing something. We try to avoid that.'

I am reminded frequently that Emirati society in Abu Dhabi can be brutal. 'We are few, we may not know who a person is right away, but we will probably know the family and so we make connections.' I don't remember being 'out' with Emirati women anywhere in the city when we haven't seen people who are recognized, sometimes acknowledged and always talked about. Because I have now taught, advised and worked with so many of the young women of Abu Dhabi, it is now impossible for me to go anywhere without soon hearing my name called out by current and former students, their sisters, cousins and other relatives. It is indeed a small place. 'Before life changed, the families lived close together. Even with the first houses, the *buyut al shaabiyya*, the *freej* [traditional neighborhoods] were mostly family and for sure they were only one tribe. Now we have Manasir living side by side with Dhawahir and Qubaisat, and so it has all changed. We used to be able to walk freely around, visiting, shopping—women used to sell fish in the market! Can you imagine that happening now? No, now we are stuck behind these walls.'

Abu Dhabi is a city of walls. Walls surround the palaces of the ruling family; the extended family compounds that have houses for each of the sons and their families; and the relatively rare single villa. The palaces and compounds are enormous and include manicured gardens, garages for multiple cars, rooms and facilities for the domestic servants, and a *majlis* or two, separate from the houses, for receiving guests and entertaining family and friends during Ramadan and Eid. The gardens often sound like a menagerie, especially in the mornings when the trees are alive with collections of exotic birds that fly freely when they wish to leave the safety of their aviary.

Driving into a family compound requires caution. In addition to the animal population there are usually quite a few children running about during cooler weather. The park-like gardens are put to hard use by children riding bikes, rollerblading, jumping on trampolines, digging in flowerbeds, climbing trees and chasing after each other through the grass. It is in a hard-used garden that I sit with five women in the coolness of a February morning. Four of the women are related and the one who is not has been so close to the family that she is '*khalti*', aunt, too, out of both love and respect. They have just finished their weekly Quran lesson in which they are all striving to improve their pronunciation and understanding. Convinced that I too should take the class, they haven't quite decided how to get around the fact that as a non-believer, albeit an *ahl al kitab*, a person whose faith shares the knowledge and revelations of the Abrahamic tradition, I shouldn't be touching the Quran. And then too there is the question of me being able to understand the true meaning, because that is only made manifest for believers. I am a little more practical and know that I wouldn't be able to attend their Quran class with my schedule as it is, even if they resolved the difficulties to their satisfaction.

We talk that day about religion, life and community. I have kept them up to date with all the discussions and projects in my classes and they have much to add. One of their shared concerns is that there is no feeling of community any more—at least not the sort that they remember from their childhood and would like to have again. Their ages range from early thirties to early fifties and so memories of community vary, but all agree that it was 'better' and 'closer' in the past. I suggest quite timidly, given that the women around me are nothing if not blunt, that perhaps the loss of community is just one of the side-effects of a growing and now more mobile population. Yes and no. 'Certainly, some things have changed because that is life nowadays. And you are right, our population has increased and that means that we are spread out across the city in new areas.' Reem, the eldest, thinks a bit longer. 'I think it is more than that, our 'community' as you call it no longer really exists—now we are *ijtima'a*, a society, and that is new still—especially all the bad things that come with it.' Reem goes on to list what she perceives to be the bad things. 'Well, first we are divided now; we are not, as I think we used to be, just families, clans and tribes; now we are classes of people. There is the ruling family;

there are the very rich that are attached to them, less rich but still rich; then I guess what you would call upper middle class; and then we have lower class people. Those are the ones no one ever talks about.' The others chime in before she can finish her list of bad things. 'And drugs and alcohol!' 'And men abandoning their wives and children!' 'And everyone competing to show off, like at weddings!' The list was long and the discussion grew heated as they argued about which was worse, what the causes were and what would happen in the future.

'Shopping and weddings, they fill up our days'

Their discussion and others have made it clear that many Emiratis are critical of what they perceive to be new standards and statuses. The new standards are luxury, designer labels, and consumption on a grand, often unbelievable scale. A walk through any of the malls in the country is evidence of the market in all things expensive that exists in the UAE. Designer goods that, in the US at least, would be attached to a large department store such as Nordstrom or Neiman Marcus, or clustered together on 5th Avenue or Rodeo Drive, are displayed in single-design/label shops in just about every mall. DG, Jimmy Choo, Fendi, Burberry, Chanel and Dior are favorites. One acquaintance was told that Armani was the only thing that men should wear, so she promptly gave all her husband's 'Western clothes' to charity and purchased an entire Armani wardrobe for him. The cost was staggering but her husband was not concerned about the money, he was angry that she had thrown out his favorite old cardigan!

Shopping with Emirati women is depressing. There is no other way to describe the experience of standing next to someone who has never worked a day in her life, and may well not ever, as she casually tosses a platinum credit card on the counter and spends thousands of dollars without even blinking or, in fact, looking at the total as she signs the slip. Jewelry shopping with Emirati women defies description. Any who are seriously in the market for jewelry don't go shopping; the jeweler comes to them. Tall black cases arrive at the door and are ushered into the sitting area where the women are gathered, waiting. The jewelry is Harry Winston, Van Cleef and Arpels and Tiffany. Jewelry shopping usually precedes a big wedding celebration for which everything that is worn has to be new.

Preparations for weddings can be somewhat tense. Everyone seems to know when and where the wedding celebration will be, long before an invitation arrives. Once an engagement is official and the marriage contract has been agreed upon, a date is selected and a venue chosen. Sometimes the venue is chosen before the marriage contract has been signed in order to make sure that an adequately sized venue is available. Word of the wedding celebration then circulates through aunts and cousins to friends. Dresses are ordered first, both because they take time and because the 'good tailors' will be busy in the weeks running up to a really big wedding. Once the design and the fabric for the dresses have been selected, then the shoes, bags and jewelry are purchased. I now know that US$ 10,000 is not an unreasonable price for a Fendi bag.

See, be seen, and surpass

The sums of money spent on Emirati weddings can be staggering. The wedding celebrations of the wealthy families are lavish events with big name entertainment such as Muhammad Abdu, Amr Diab and Jasmi. Full dinners are served and there are usually substantial gifts for all the guests. The venues are hotel ballrooms and now, for the more prominent families, several thousand square feet of the Abu Dhabi National Exhibition Center. These spaces are transformed into a fantasy world of lights, flower arrangements, decorations, stages and fountains. These transformations are increasingly 'themed' by an army of decorators and wedding directors who create Zen gardens, tropical rainforests, modern Roman forums and 'a thousand and one nights' fantasies, complete with a runway down the middle of the table area for the bride to take her walk so that everyone can admire her dress. Wedding dresses, white in the Western style, can cost more than a million *dirhams*. One of my students interrupted her final semester twice to fly to Paris for fittings, and the dress, a Pierre Cardin, surely exceeded a million *dirhams* even without figuring in the trips to Paris.

The elaborately adorned tables at weddings are set with crystal goblets, fine china and linen napkins. Droves of attendants make sure that each table is perfect. Enormous platters of food appear, and some are so laden, so heavy, that they must be wheeled out on carts; the rest are carried around by two attendants while two more serve guests, making round after round of the tables. Likewise, huge trays of Belgian chocolates and rich pastries circle constantly among the tables. *Qahwa*, the cardamom-spiced coffee favored by Emiratis, is poured into tiny porcelain cups by women whose only job is to make sure that everyone is greeted immediately with a cup and that none of us will be without the offer of another for the entire evening. At some weddings, if it is Emirati women who serve the coffee, they wear an *'abayah* decorated with a golden *dallah*, the Emirati coffee pot with its distinctive long spout. Young camels are served, as is goat. In addition to traditional foods such as *harees* and *biryani*, often *kibbeh*, *fattoush*, *waraq ainab* and other rather generic foods of the Middle East are included. There are so many foods, so many sweets, so many glasses of fresh juice, so many chocolates and so many cups of coffee that it is amazing. Few guests actually eat. They may sample the *harees* or the camel or try a piece of chocolate but they do not eat the food that has been placed on their plate. Women hold up the *burqah* with the thumb and forefinger of their left hand in order to sip *qahwa* and juices, and they will do the same to sample something else.

Weddings have become highly competitive and appear to have codified rules of engagement for what some of my students have called 'the battles of the mothers' and the intricate set of norms which are used to measure and judge not only the success of a wedding but the dress, decorum and status of all the guests.

Location is critical. The venue itself is loaded with connotations. First, certain venues are 'in' and others are 'out'. As Abu Dhabi has grown, so have the choices for weddings. Five years ago most weddings that I attended were at the Intercontinental Hotel, but no longer; now notable weddings are at the Emirates Palace Hotel or the Abu Dhabi National Exhibition Center. Having a wedding in either of those venues immediately communicates that there will be lots of guests and that it cost lots of money. When invitations arrived to the first wedding to be held at the Exhibition Center they were greeted with scorn. Women who were attending were critical and suspect. 'Is it to be a wedding or an exhibition?' 'No place else was big enough for their wedding? What is this about?' After that first wedding it now seems that the Exhibition Center is the place and that it is rivaled only by the Emirates Palace. 'Emirates Palace is much nicer of course, and you don't have to design a whole space there, but it can only hold so many people.' Access to the Exhibition Center too is a plus because drivers can drop passengers at the door to the one (or two) halls reserved for weddings well within the complex, and so arrivals are relatively private.

Arrivals are important. The order in which cars arrive when women come in large groups is also important. The senior women of the family arrive at the wedding first. The short journey from a house in the Mushref area to the Exhibition Center got dangerously complicated as drivers were told to pull off to the side of the road and wait until the 'lead car,' carrying the most senior of the women in the group, had taken its position. Once at the Exhibition Center, our caravan of five cars waited until the area in front of the entry steps was completely clear of other guests, and then the drivers pulled our cars forward so that all the women of the family could disembark in unison. The timing of arriving in proper order is complicated when weddings are held in hotel banquet rooms, because often there is a short drop-off point near the front of the hotel. The drivers must know the order in which the women want to disembark, get all the cars in line in the proper order and manage to fend off other drivers who try to jump the queue. How one disembarks from the car is also important, as is how one mounts the steps to the entry door. This part of the arrival is more critical for young, unmarried women because they are under intense scrutiny as possible future brides. Arriving or entering with hair exposed is taken as immodesty even if the poor girl's *shaylah* has been blown off by a gust of wind. I rarely see a *shaylah* wrapped and tucked so tight as when we are getting out of a car at a wedding. The first steps into the actual wedding may be marred by security complete with walk-through metal detectors and efforts to relieve the guests of their mobile phones. Mobile phones with cameras are the target for

79

the security people as there is fear that pictures taken can then be sent surreptitiously via Bluetooth and SMS to all and sundry. I have been told that this has indeed happened. Pictures of young ladies, dressed and made up for a wedding, had been sent and then re-sent to thousands of mobile numbers. Taking away mobiles is rarely successful and everyone with whom I have attended weddings takes great umbrage at the security overlay. 'It seems we can't compete on dresses or gifts any more, so now you have to impress people with this nonsense.' Amna's comment is a bit exaggerated, because security measures are usually put in place when someone from the ruling family is expected. Her Highness Sheikha Fatima bint Mubarak, the widow of Sheikh Zayed bin Sultan, is probably invited to every wedding in the city, and so optimistic families put on security just in case she might arrive.

What is classified as a big wedding changes with each wedding. What is big is also notable, meaning that it involves at least one and most probably two very wealthy families, or two branches of the same wealthy family. A really big wedding is one within the ruling family. Wedding celebrations are enormously expensive and unbelievably elaborate. The money spent on these celebrations is often cited as the reason why Emirati men choose to marry non-Emiratis. Women don't agree with that, although they might admit that weddings are extraordinarily exorbitant. They typically point to the weddings of the ruling families as the cause. 'Of course they set the standard for these things. Everyone watches and takes notice of their weddings. We notice the food, the decorations, how many guests are invited, the gifts, the music, the entertainment and even the table cloths! We notice and we remember.' The woman speaking has boycotted the last three of these weddings because she objects, on principle, to VIP seating and the security measures, like metal detectors and female guards, which distinguish such affairs. When I remind her of this she tells me that she didn't have to go; she got full reports from her sisters and friends. 'I refuse to go along with this separation of people! Who is and who is not a VIP? It is ridiculous. Forty years ago we would have all been in the same big cluster of tents sitting on cushions! Now we are 'royals' with hangers on and groupies, VIPs and security. Who, I ask you, is going to threaten a *sheikha* at a wedding!? It is all just a big show. Look, this is the way we do it now that we are so rich—we can make you go through our security and you will sit where we tell you to sit. Not me.' I am a little surprised at this because I know, having been to several weddings with her, that she is always and unequivocally seated in the VVIP section.

'The competition is ferocious, that's the only way to describe it.' Hissa and I are having coffee after shopping at the Abu Dhabi mall. 'Weddings are about the only time that women get to compete, so of course it is a big deal.' We talk about the last wedding that we both attended as one of the truly big weddings, held at the Abu Dhabi National Exhibition Center. Hissa remarks that just the location says it all: 'They are an exhibition!' But surely there are other avenues, other arenas for competition among women, I insist. 'Like what? They barely let us compete against each other in sports in high school! Compete for good grades? Compete for good jobs? That doesn't even register.' I counter with several examples of very competitive students. 'Your students are the younger generation; I'm talking about my generation—their mothers!' Hissa went on to explain her perspective on the difference between her mother's life, the life she is living and the lives that her daughters have now and will have in the future. Her mother's generation was made up of strong women, she says. They were strong women who worked, gave birth alone in the desert, ran farms and sold fish in the markets. Hissa continues. 'When the development started, after oil was found, these women were involved with the building of the country. They pushed for literacy programs so they could learn to read, they joined Sheikha Fatima's Association for Local Women, they insisted that all of their children go to school, and they argued for equal rights for women if they chose to work. They were involved.' I ask about her generation. Hissa smiles but her tone is serious. 'My generation is the lazy one, the one that got everything too fast. We don't know how to cook, we have let maids and nannies raise our children, we have never worked and we spend our entire day shopping, thinking about shopping or talking on the phone. We are a wasted generation really.' 'But surely not,' I argue. 'There are many women in their late forties and fifties who are involved, who have meaningful jobs and are taking an active part in the development of society.' 'No, there are a few, but not many. The majority of my generation of women have had children; that is our contribution to society.'

Months later we return to this topic with other women. 'You know, I don't even know how to find things in Abu Dhabi! I have always had a driver and I just expect the driver to know where it is I want to go.' I can sympathize with her because I have been witnessing the utter chaos that resulted when one family's driver left for two months. Of course they had a substitute driver, borrowed from another branch of the family. 'He doesn't know where anything is!' The women of the family, none of whom drive, were prisoners in the house because they couldn't give directions to the substitute driver.

'It is the same with traveling in the summer. We can't travel without a maid or two—how would we cope? I don't dress my children here, much less wash their clothes—how would I do that in Switzerland?' As families prepare for the summer holidays in Europe and America, one of the big decisions to make is which one (or two) of the maids will be coming along. 'We cannot take Hala, she will run for sure!' 'Filipinas don't usually run away so we take them.' Runaway maids are an ugly business. It is socially embarrassing because 'it would automatically be assumed that we were bad to her.' It also draws the family, or at least the husband, into the legal system of another country when the maid is reported missing.[1] I have been told there is an underground network in London that aids women who have run away from their employers. 'I think they have a telephone number that they call first and then arrangements are made. You know one summer a few years back all of the maids—and I think they had four—ran away at the same time!! They had to come back home right away because how could they cope?' This is a somewhat thorny topic and not one that I am comfortable discussing because it is impossible for me to sound even the slightest bit sympathetic. Fortunately for all concerned, the number of runaway maids has decreased in the last few years and so while maids are still selected carefully before summer travel, there have been no tales to hear in September.

5

MARRIAGE, EDUCATION AND CHOICES

I can raise no topic in class that instantly prompts as loud and passionate discussion as does that of marriage. My students expect to get married and want to stay married despite the UAE's soaring divorce rate, which is the highest in the Gulf (Al Awadhi 2007). Marriage and children are critical to a woman's status and there are but a few notable figures like Sheikha Lubna al Qasimi, the Minister of Foreign Trade, who are publicly single. This is not to imply that women are not present in the government. There are two ambassadors, four cabinet ministers, a judge, and eight of the forty representatives in the Federal National Council are women (UAE 2009). Historically women accessed power and influence by virtue of their role as wife and mother (Soffan 1980:40). Sheikha Hussa bint al Murra was a powerful women who held her own public *majlis*, was a trader and businesswoman and wielded great influence in Dubai, but that is of less significance than the fact that she was the wife of the ruler, Sheikh Sa'eed, and the grandmother of Sheikh Mohammad bin Rashid al Maktoum, the current ruler of Dubai. Similarly, Sheikha Maitha bint Salmeen, who donned men's clothes and fought on horseback to protect her tribe's property and honor, is remembered but probably because she then married Sheikh Zayed the Great, who ruled Abu Dhabi in the nineteenth and early twentieth centuries.

Emirati parents straddle what they perceive to be an uncomfortable and dangerous divide. On the one side are government policies

83

that encourage women to participate actively in the public life of the nation. Media rhetoric extols the contributions of working women and now those who have been elected to the Federal National Council as political representatives. On that same side are their educated and talented daughters who want careers and an opportunity to contribute. On the other side of the divide are the cultural norms that help define a woman's role as wife and mother.

University education has been a significant factor in the rising marriage age of Emirati women, and it also contributes to perceptions of worth and value in the marriage market. Tertiary education is now so prevalent, thanks to government encouragement in the form of free tuition for citizens, that it is actually the lack of a degree or diploma that will have an effect on a woman's marriage prospects. Worse still is the adverse impact of failing at university studies, and great pains are taken to conceal that fact when a student must leave university. If she leaves under a dark cloud, such as being expelled for bad behavior or lacking academic integrity—as cheating is now called—her family will most probably make direct and personal appeals for reinstatement, sometimes to members of the ruling family. In the manner of most parents, it is the institution or the bad influence of friends that is blamed for the situation, not their daughter. A dismissed student—and I have not known of any whose parents' appeals were successful if their dismissal was warranted, regardless of their social standing—is not eligible for admission to any other nationally funded institution. Her parents may choose to enroll their daughter at a private university and pay the tuition, but in those cases familiar to me this has happened only twice. Much more commonly, before the news of her dismissal has spread too far into the Emirati community, the girl is engaged to be married within a week or two.

Opinions about marriage and divorce vary according to age. Parents and grandparents say that they still think an arranged marriage is best because both sides of the family will be supportive and that gives the new couple a better chance of success. They, like parents and grandparents everywhere, also think that they know best, and if not best at least better than any twenty-year-old woman. The frequency of what are called 'love matches' has increased since women are in the workplace in greater numbers. Forty years ago a young woman would have had little opportunity to meet, much less talk to, a man from outside the family. Now offices, colleges and universities—despite the segregation imposed in some—provide opportunities to meet and talk to members of the opposite sex outside of the home. Most mothers seem to take this in their stride and say that the world has changed now; one has to get used to it. 'No sense getting all that education if she isn't going to use it by working,' says Hamda about her daughter. 'I trust her; she is not going to be stupid and gullible.'

Surprisingly it is often the young women who draw back at the idea of 'being around men,' not their parents. The university has a women-only campus, but that does not mean that men are not present. In fact, at least half of the faculty is male. Males are present too in the shape of custodians, repairmen, administration, drivers and gardeners, but those men are not a factor because (with the exception of one or two upper administrators) they are not Emirati men. Our students complete a ten-week internship period in their senior year, and the prospect of having to work alongside Emirati men is worrisome to most of them. 'But what will I do? How will I handle being in the same office as a man?' I assure each batch of new interns that everything will be fine, that it will feel strange at first and that the men will be accustomed to working around women so they will be professional. After a flurry of consultations that determine what everyone else is wearing for the first day, internship begins with a tone of mild hysteria. In my experience, the hysteria wears off by the end of the second day and then I hear, 'Oh, yeah, Muhammad, he's okay, but rather nerdy, like a brother.' By the end of the first week all is well, though they may still balk at sharing an office with an Emirati man. So far, after years of internships, I know of lots of job offers but no engagements have developed.

The hot topics for young Emirati women and their mothers are whether the marriage should be arranged by the family or be a 'love match' that may or may not be considered suitable, who cannot be married no matter what, what kind of wedding to have, and life after marriage. The whole marriage complex weighs heavily on my students' minds, but they are often more concerned with the state of marriage in the Emirates generally than with their own. Thirty years ago the age of marriage for women was around fifteen or sixteen and sometimes younger depending on the family (Soffan 1980:33). Education and new opportunities have since changed that and now eighteen is considered quite young and the more common age is twenty-two, typically after the woman has graduated from university. Of course, this is a generalization as some women become engaged before they graduate and a few do marry while studying at university. Some marry even younger, when in high school.[1] Some of my students are married and a few balance pregnancy and children with their studies, but it is more common to announce the engagement in the last year of study with the wedding then held after graduation. However, there are enough women not marrying at any age to have caused concern, both on the part of young women who are not engaged and on the part of government officials (Bristol-Rhys 2007). The prospect of spinsterhood is ominous in a society that puts great value on marriage and the family and one in which a woman's status is still inextricably linked to her role of wife and mother.

Exactly how many Emirati women might be considered to be spinsters is hard to pinpoint as statistics are not available. I say might be considered because the definition of spinster is not clear. A woman who has refused offers of marriage may be considered a spinster in some situations and by some people but not all. Aunts and grandmothers appear to support the decision to refuse a proposal, and in two cases known to me they convinced the young woman that she should refuse. One young friend refused two proposals with the full support of her grandmother and maternal aunts because they all knew that she was waiting for a particular cousin. A woman who is intent upon building a career may say that she is postponing marriage, but the older women in her family may exert pressure on her to accept a marriage proposal soon and then postpone the marriage for a year or two. As the age of marriage has been rising, so too has the age associated with the onset of spinsterhood. Judging by talk among women and the occasional raised eyebrow, it appears that twenty-seven is the precipice and if a woman is not married by that age she is in peril. A twenty-three-year-old woman in graduate school does not prompt concern, but a twenty-five-year-old who works, drives her own car and is not engaged will probably be the subject of gossip.

There are several interrelated factors that have caused this to be such a contentious issue for women. As I mentioned earlier, the pressure to marry is uniformly intense across Emirati society, and unmarried women are viewed as somewhat incomplete no matter how successful they might be in other endeavors. A significant portion of this social pressure stems from strongly held religious conviction that marriage is essential both for the individual and for the well-being of the society. No acceptable relationships exist outside of marriage. Unmarried women remain legally dependent on their father or brothers, and in some cases this means that their social world is circumscribed by their natal family.[2] It would be rare for an Emirati woman to consider or be allowed to live away from her family, in her own apartment or sharing with a friend, and so if she does not marry she will continue to stay at home and guardianship will pass from her father when he dies to her oldest brother.

'Emirati men are marrying foreign women instead of us'

The complexity of marriage is compounded by the fact that Emirati women are expected, indeed required, to marry Emirati men. This may sound like an inordinately obvious proposition on the whole, but it is not quite so clear-cut because Emirati men can marry anyone they wish regardless of nationality or religion.[3] Women are very conscious of the double standard inherent in the public discourse on Emirati marriage, and also express frustration because they feel powerless to change the situation. It is not fair, they say, that men can marry foreign women and so legally bestow Emirati citizenship on them and their children, while if an Emirati woman marries an outsider her children will not be given citizenship but will be considered to be as foreign as their father. Emirati women may marry citizens of the other Gulf countries but children born of the marriage may be legally Bahraini or Kuwaiti, not Emirati. This the women see to be ridiculously stupid when the government hands out rewards for having many children in an attempt to increase the population. They also point to the fact that while Emiratis publically bemoan the adverse impact that non-Arabic speaking maids and nannies are having on children's language and cultural identity, no one is brave enough to confront the issue when it involves non-Arabic speaking mothers who are wives to Emirati men.

According to Emirati women, the men of the country have been exercising the legal right to marry foreign women all too frequently, and for many this is the root of the spinsterhood problem. Again, it is impossible to guess at the numbers involved as accurate nationwide statistics are not available, but the frequency of Emirati men marrying non-Emirati women has been sufficient to warrant media coverage and changes made to the criteria that a man must meet in order to receive a government-funded marriage subsidy. The Marriage Fund was set up by Sheikh Zayed in 1992. This agency is funded to award cash grants to Emirati men to help them pay the *mahr*, or bride price, so that they can afford to marry an Emirati woman. The amount of cash varies with the financial situation of the applicant up to a maximum amount of 70,000 *dirham*, about US$ 20,000. In 1992 the monthly salary of an applicant could be no higher than 13,000 *dirham* (US$ 3,500) but that figure was raised to 16,000 *dirham* (US$ 4,600) in 2003 (Bristol-Rhys 2007).

While media reporting on the issue has been significant and constant for the last thirty years, it has not been directly critical of Emirati men. In fact, much of the media commentary connects the inflationary and spiraling amount of *mahr*, the cash, jewelry and other gifts that are expected by families as bride price, to an Emirati man's decision to marry a non-Emirati woman. *Mahr* represents security for the woman in the case of divorce or the death of her husband, and a significant portion of what is given is to be the bride's personal wealth. Oftentimes the *mahr* is actually divided into two disbursements, the second portion being withheld for a couple of years in case of a divorce (Soffan 1980:33). While religious guidance from the Hadith of the Prophet Muhammad promotes a reasonable *mahr* that should not be burdensome, and in fact the *mahr* can be purely symbolic such as teaching someone to read the Quran, the great wealth of Emirati society has inflated expectations about an acceptable *mahr*.

The costs of wedding celebrations have skyrocketed too, and because a portion of the *mahr* is intended to cover some expenses of the wedding celebration, the two functions have become conflated and it is common to hear the word *mahr* used to refer to wedding costs generally (Soffan 1980:33). This is the use of the term *mahr* when it is cited in the newspapers as the rationale to marry non-Emirati women. There are many narratives about marriage. To marry an Emirati is too expensive and so, we are told, finding no other alternative, an Emirati man is forced to marry a foreigner. I know of no one who actually believes this, including Emirati men. They do talk about money when marriage comes up in conversation, but more frequently than not it is about how much it will cost to support an Emirati wife, not what it will cost to marry her. 'They are spoiled, all of them. They are used to having whatever they want no matter how silly or how expensive. Their father may have the money to spend on them but what will I do on my salary?' This young man, Abdullah, wants to get married and he wants to marry an Emirati but he is concerned that money will become a bone of contention with his wife. Emirati women have full control of their own money, whether from their father or an earned salary. Wives are not expected to contribute funds to the household; that is entirely the man's responsibility. As with most expectations, this is negotiable and couples usually work out compromises. One young couple uses the wife's salary for their vacation fund, a tutor for their young daughter and contributions to their 'gift giving account.' Others make similar agreements about money such as putting baby clothes on the wife's side of the ledger, while the husband pays for an extra maid or nanny to help with the kids.

Abdullah's comment that Emirati women are used to having the best of everything is commonly heard in these narratives about marriage, and so too are those that claim Emirati mothers-in-law are too meddlesome. Not surprisingly, such comments upset my friends and their retort is that Emirati men are shunning them because foreign women are more easily dominated generally, and more so because they have no family to protect them here in the UAE. The interference men complain about is, say the women, their parents' insistence that their husband treats them with respect.

Women from countries such as Malaysia, Indonesia and the Philippines who are frequently chosen as wives are described as 'docile' and 'subservient' by Emirati women. 'They don't expect to be treated like we do and they will put up with nonsense like staying out all night, going to bad places and being a bad husband.'

The fact that Emirati men often choose women from poorer countries is proof positive for many of the women I have spoken to that 'these men don't want wives and families. They want maids that have no rights and no family protection and, oh yes, they want sex but not the responsibilities that come with a family.' Comments like these are common in the women's narratives about men marrying foreigners and reflect increasing concern that South Asian and South-East Asian women, many of whom enter the country as domestic servants and retail workers, are opportunists looking to marry an Emirati man in order to escape the poverty of their home countries. Such comments may also be indicative that Emirati women are objectifying domestic workers, turning them into the 'other' who has evil intentions and cannot be trusted (Anderson 2000:147).

'Never hire a Moroccan maid'

As a Western woman with the 'it takes two to tango' school of thought, it is hard for me to fathom how it is that Emirati women don't get angrier at Emirati men. They blame the women whom they tend to describe as gold diggers who 'take jobs as maids so that they can steal the husband away when the wife isn't looking.' I am not at all sure how it is that Moroccan women specifically have been able to earn the ire of Emirati women generally, but they have. The mere mention of 'Moroccan maid' ignites women with anecdotes and stories of seduction and perfidy. This is not confined to students either, and I have been told completely and utterly unbelievable tales by Emirati women of all ages. I have never, however, met a Moroccan woman who has an Emirati husband. There is a special brand of venomous criticism reserved for Lebanese women as well. 'Dressing like a Lebanese' has become a euphemism for wearing too much make-up, tight and revealing clothes, with the presumed intention of luring a man.

It is interesting to note that there is the general perception by Emirati women that the women—no matter what their country of origin—who married Emirati men twenty or more years ago were not opportunistic. It is men choosing to marry foreigners now who are causing problems, and it appears that current discourse revolves around the presumption that it is economics that motivates women to marry Emirati men today. Class discussions on who can marry whom and why foreign women want to marry Emirati men quickly focus on the economic benefits. The loudest discussion is about the number of foreign women in the country who, according to the vast majority of my students over the years, are all intent on 'catching' an Emirati man. None of them has ever argued, persuasively or otherwise, that Emirati men are the best men in the world and therefore sought after by all women. Nor do they argue that Emirati men choose to marry foreign women because they just want to—perhaps because love is involved. No, the students all presume that foreign women are calculating and methodical in the hunt for a rich Emirati man. While some of the students might admit that not every single foreign female has come to the UAE in a premeditated search for an Emirati husband (I always thank them for that acknowledgment), as a group they agree that 'something happens' that makes the women start 'hunting.' 'They see the cars, they see the clothes, they see the good life and they want it.' And so, I ask, they set out to find the first Emirati male and just bat their eyes at him and he agrees to marry? I am assured that it is much more devious than that. 'Where do these women meet Emirati men?' I ask. 'Oh, just about everywhere. They meet the women when they are at work in the shops. They meet them in coffee shops and restaurants. Emirati men can go everywhere and those women do too!'

I am on rather thin ice here because I am never quite sure what my students know about the steamier side of Abu Dhabi that includes bars, prostitutes and lots of other illicit and illegal activities. I used to think that they all lived rather secluded if not cloistered lives, but that is far from the truth. Boyfriends are common, and complicated arrangements for clandestine meetings through accommodating aunts and complicit drivers make for an interesting and active social life. Some years ago I adopted a 'don't ask, don't tell' stance with regard to what students and former students were up to, but even with that, I know too much. I am impressed with the amount of planning, creativity and downright deviousness that is necessary to meet and keep a boyfriend, but more concerned about what will happen if the relationship is discovered. I did get caught up in one particularly cunning plan to meet the boyfriend that was, I found out too late, orchestrated around a fieldtrip to Dubai that would end with a short excursion to the Mall of the Emirates. I was impressed with the intricate planning, but also angry because it was an official trip.

I have been used as a foil for buying presents too. 'While we are here, I want to go look at cufflinks' sounds innocent enough until I realize that the cufflinks are not for Dad. 'Let's go look at the new Nokia mobile phones; I might want to get one.' The phone is purchased and then arrangements are made to have it delivered. Across the city of Abu Dhabi there are lots of mothers who must think that I have an enormous stash of IPods, mobile phones, car gadgets and a complete collection of all the latest Khaleeji music gifted to me by their daughters. I hope they don't ask.

When the discussion calms down somewhat, I ask how many of their uncles and brothers have foreign wives; their responses are telling. In a class of twenty or thirty students one or two may acknowledge that a male relative has married a non-Emirati. Once we establish that perhaps the rate of Emirati men marrying foreign women is not as alarming as they thought, then we set to analyzing the narrative and exploring the perceptions that underlie it.

At the fundamental level is the perception that Emirati men have access to all of Abu Dhabi and that women do not; the repeated complaint about access and mobility. Emirati men can indeed go everywhere; Emirati women cannot. 'We go to shops and the malls, that's it. But look around you! Hotels are now everywhere. That is where the men go. We can't go in there at all, for any reason.' Hotels, even the public lobbies, are off-limits for many students, except in the case of an exhibition. 'The hotels are monuments to foreigners,' say students who often characterize hotels as foreign havens of liquor and licentiousness. Women describe the city's hotels as dangerous places to be seen unless you are from an exceptional family that just doesn't care. Women tell me that men don't have the same restrictions placed on their activities and so do use hotel coffee shops as meeting places. However, there is the underlying insinuation that the only bona fide reason to go to a hotel is to meet with foreign business contacts. Just hanging around a hotel is perceived to be bad or proto-bad behavior. This extends to groups of Emirati men too. If we see a group of Emirati men sitting together at a table in one of the lobby areas at the Emirates Palace when we are there for an exhibit, the students assume the worst and avoid that area assiduously.

Consequently there are few Emiratis to be seen in the hotels around town, and when they are present they draw attention from tourists who quickly spot the crisp white *kandoura* worn by the men and the black *'abayah* of the women. I have been forced to intervene when normally Western tourists train their cameras on my students, apparently under the impression that the sudden and fortuitous appearance of Emiratis must be another stage-managed benefit of staying at the Palace. The students are a bit shocked and quite angry to be so confronted by what they see to be unforgivably bad behavior. When I point out that the tourists might not yet have encountered an Emirati woman they are hardly mollified. 'What are we? Freaks on display?'

The fact that men can go to hotels and, presumably, the bars and nightclubs that are located there is just one example of the unequal access to the 'new Abu Dhabi' that women discuss.[4] In fact, I am frequently asked whom I see when I am at hotels. 'What do they do there? Are they drinking in the bar?' Thankfully I have never run into anyone's husband, brother or son! Most of the city's bars have discrete signs at the entry to remind clients that 'national dress' is not appropriate and, therefore, Emirati men who do choose to go inside should not be wearing immediately recognizable clothing. Even more discrete, so much so that it is confusing to tourists, are those signs that 'prohibit entry to men wearing sandals' because Emirati men typically wear sandals with their *kandoura*, this being a way to get the message across without mentioning national dress.

Access and freedom of movement is about much more than hotels, and I don't mean to imply that there are dozens of Emirati women waiting impatiently to be allowed into a bar, because there aren't. Access is also about the ability to confront, to make a stand, to argue one's case and to complain. I have never seen my friends happier than when a toll-free consumer complaint center was launched. Mobile phones were suddenly being whipped out of purses and brandished in front of clerks and store managers. 'This is the best thing because we don't have to go into an office and make our complaint.' I asked if it was because of the anonymity. 'No, no, I give my name, we all do. Who I am isn't the issue; it is complaining, or making the complaint in an office, that we can't do.' Why they cannot, or rather believe they cannot, go to an office is confusing. Some women tell me that it is not appropriate behavior for a woman to confront a man, and since they assume that it will be men in the offices, they do not go. I point out that more and more women are working in the government offices so that may not be an issue any more. The response is the same: it is unseemly for a woman to do business like that. 'In fact, women shouldn't show anger or strong emotion in public at all,' says Alyazia. 'We are raised that way. It is okay to yell at the kids at home, but you never raise your voice to your father or uncles.' I get a smile when I ask about raising your voice to your husband. 'Well, that has to be done sometimes! But never to older males in your family; that is not our way.' The city of Abu Dhabi has now launched a website for the public to air complaints and offer suggestions.[5] This people can do in both Arabic and English. It is probably safe to bet that they will be hearing from Emirati women in the hundreds; my friends are already registering their thoughts.

In the case of serious issues like traffic accidents, bank account foul-ups, visas for travel and so forth, most women seem to involve their brothers or sons, not their husbands. Some of this of course might reflect the brother's status and reputation, and in some cases it is the brothers' jobs that put them in a position to be ready problem-solvers. However, in most cases that I have observed, it appears to be almost reflex action; sisters are used to calling on their brothers for help. I have heard brothers groan loudly on the other end of the phone, but not one has told his sister 'no.' Husbands, of course, deal with the crises that involve the house and the family: visas for drivers and maids, car and house maintenance. Since the husbands are, in most cases, also cousins of the brothers, I have wondered how much is shared between the men. Several incidents indicate that brothers keep quiet and, I assume, husbands have learned not to ask. A recent car wreck set off waves of phone calls, starting with the girl's mother calling her brother. There was swift intervention by the brother not only to extricate his niece from dealing with police by the side of the road but also to have the totaled car replaced with a brand new one in less than 24 hours. I don't think the husband/father knows still.

Brothers are also asked to intervene on the behalf of people they have never met but who somehow have crossed the paths of their sisters, and in some cases their mothers. 'A'eeb, this is shameful! They need to have a bigger house! You must do something. You must get them a bigger house.' I happened to be sitting with the women of one family when the discussion turned to a recent visit by a widow whose house was too small to accommodate the wives and families of her sons. The woman was not particularly close to the family and had come to the house in the company of some distant cousins. I did not hear her ask for help with her house or even complain about her situation. Ten minutes after the visiting women left the conversation turned to the widow and her situation. The women all expressed concern about the size of her house and the importance of keeping her sons around. 'Mansour will get them a new house!' announced Mansour's mother, and his sisters all agreed. Mansour was less enthusiastic when he was told this on the phone, but he promised to investigate. A week later I was told that Mansour had in fact been able to help by advising the son access the government-funded housing program.

Brothers are also chaperones for their
though it seems that they agree
are younger than the sister, in wh
dents who need extra guidance or
to meet me at one of the malls for c
out of ten bring along a brother. Go
even if you are going to meet a bor.
friends and students for shopping or

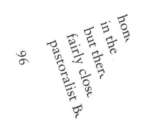

mall or, if they are being dropped off by the driver, I wait just inside the entry doors and then step out to meet them. It is rare indeed to see an Emirati woman alone in a mall or a shop. Women with children are relatively common, as are groups of three or more young women together. A friend and I were walking through the front of a restaurant to our seats in the back one day and we both stopped dead in our tracks; there was an Emirati woman sitting alone at a table and she was smoking. We were both stunned and we stared quite rudely. We recovered from the shock and continued to our table, but we were still incredulous. 'Who can she be?' I suggested that we were mistaken, that she wasn't Emirati but one of those women who dressed as if they were. 'No, no, she is for sure Emirati. I can tell by the way she has her *shaylah*. And the *'abayah*, women don't spend thousands to pretend to be Emirati.' She craned her neck to have another look at the solitary figure in black. 'She is the real thing but she must have lost her mind!'

Honor and shame are tangible concepts, although both are difficult to define and explain. I have been accused of being more conservative than mothers because I gasp audibly when I hear tales of what daughters and cousins have been doing. Class discussions on the meaning and value of honor as it functions in Emirati society today usually end up with examples of shameful behavior instead. Honor, they know, resides with the women of the family; it is women who represent the public face of the family and it is women who pass honor to their male descendants. On the face of it, this seems contradictory given that women's access to the public is circumscribed, but here it is 'public knowledge' that is meant. If a woman has a reputation, meaning that people are talking about her behavior, this has damaged the honor of the family publicly. It is men who determine when honor has been breached and men ˙ho judge and punish.

⸚ender segregation has been, historically, one way to safeguard No contact, no harm, no foul. This was true in the past here ⸚irates and in many other areas of the Arab-Muslim world, ⸚as been variation in the degree of segregation that aligns to the differences between *badu* and *hadr*, nomadic- ⸚uin and those people who were settled in villages and towns (Abu Lughod 1986; Meneley 1996:82; Soffan 1980:18). Wealth and status are often marked socially by the ability to segregate women, because that signified that they did not have to work. In fact, segregation has become more prevalent in the UAE with the accumulation of wealth made possible by oil. Of course, one could argue that the gender segregation of schools could only have been a post-oil decision because it was only then that females began going to school.

The binary opposites of honor/shame and women/men have been argued from various points of view using ethnographic information from many societies (Abu Lughod 1986; Dresch 1989; El Guindi 1999; Wikan 1982 to list but a few). Abu Lughod argues that honor requires autonomy, something that the Awlad 'Ali in Egypt women do not have, and that modesty has become an alternative code for proper behavior (Abu Lughod 1986:79). For her, in essence, modesty is what the less powerful make do with. When I assign that chapter in classes I prepare for intense discussions. 'But it isn't that at all; modesty is Islamic, honor is tribal!!' 'Even men are to be modest; not just women, that is wrong.' So, then, how does it work here?

Modesty, I am told, is seen in many things. Of course the most obvious is dress; covering the body properly. This includes covering the neck and hair for women, as well as arms and legs. For some women this extends to hands and feet if they are expecting to be in a mixed-gender environment. For others, the face should be covered as well. Dressing modestly for men means that the arms and legs are covered unless at hard work or playing sports. I have had dozens of conversations about modesty and behavior with students and friends. Most agree that modesty begins with clothes, but that is not the whole story. 'Speech, to be modest, should never be profane or provocative. It is more than what you wear! You can dress modestly and still behave very immodestly,' Fatima smiles and then continues. 'You know what I mean. Eyes are dangerous, they are really dangerous.' Of course I have to jump on that one. 'Then why do we cover the face in such a way to make the eyes stand out? You could argue that veiling makes the eyes more alluring.' But I am told that it is not the eyes as eyes that are at issue, it is how they are

97

used. 'You could be in *hijab* completely and still flirt like mad with your eyes! And that is why modesty is about dress, but it is so much more. It is about everything, you as a person—how you carry yourself, how you speak to people, that you thank God for successes, that you are a good and humble person. That's what modesty is about and that is for everyone, not just us.' 'But what about the opposite?' I ask. 'Women who wear a sleeveless shirt don't necessarily mean to be immodest.' Fatima tells me that she believes that all skin should be covered: that for her is modest dress.

An immodest act or immodest behavior does not automatically lead to perdition but it may well lead to Liwa. Liwa is a cluster of oases deep in the desert, adjacent to the foreboding Rub al Khali, the Empty Quarter of the Arabian Peninsula, that is bereft of water and just about everything else. Whether fact or fiction, Liwa has become the euphemism that is used when a young woman has been caught doing something she shouldn't be doing. 'The Road to Liwa' means she's on dangerous ground and if she is caught she will be punished. 'Down the well' is another one where, when I heard it the first time, I was actually frightened for the woman in question because I knew that she had been sneaking out of her home at night. I pressed her friends when she disappeared from campus for several days and no one had heard from her. 'She's down the well at the farm by now.' When I looked shocked, I was assured that she might be in very deep hot water but that it wouldn't be in a well. As it turned out she had been sent to the family farm and was grounded there for more than a month. Other stories sound a little more gruesome and have evolved into urban legends. While my students may tell such tales with dramatic zeal, they are angry when 'honor killings' in other countries are reported by the media. 'That is so barbaric! What is wrong with those [insert Saudi, Turk, Jordanian or Yemeni as fits the headline]? That is just nonsense and the women in that country should rise up against it.' And yet, I have been told that honor killings are not entirely a thing of the past in the UAE. No one has given names or dates to back up their claim and the conversations end with a 'knowing look.'

Stories and looks notwithstanding, the burden of modesty and preserving the honor, or good name, of the family falls on the women. I remarked one day to an Emirati woman that I thought a man could walk down the street wearing only his *wuzzar*, the undergarment worn by Emirati men, with a blonde woman hanging on his arm and everyone would look the other way. She laughed. 'Everyone except the police, I would think. But yes, men can and do get away with horrible behavior and Emirati women are taught to put up with it.' I don't know Nourah very well; she and I have been introduced by a mutual friend who has told me that Nourah wants to practice speaking English with an American. Nourah went to university and works in Abu Dhabi. She wants to get promoted and is worried that her English language skills will hold her back. Nourah is a very thoughtful and serious young woman. After thinking for a moment or two she replies: 'Part of it is our Islamic understanding of the nature of human beings. Men are men, we are told, and they are easily led astray. When that happens we are supposed to understand and help them get on the right track again. But that is changing now; well, we women are changing. Few women that I know would put up with very much from a husband.'

Emirati women are supposed to 'marry up.' Hypergamy was the expected norm in the pre-oil days and while it may not be discussed per se, it is very rare to hear about a woman marrying into a family that is considered socially lower. This, like so many other cultural norms, has gotten a bit confusing because of the wealth which courses through Emirati society. Who is lower now? Grandmothers weigh in heavily at these times; their memories of who was who and how they were ranked are often the deciding factor. Some of the memories are tinged with old rancor and enmity. 'She would rather have me marry an Egyptian than marry someone from that family!' claims Suhaila. 'No way in the world would she let that happen, because they used to work for us; in her eyes that would be like marrying the driver, for God's sake.' When I point out that the family in question, at least the branch we are talking about, is fabulously wealthy and well-respected now, I get a look that tells me that I am incredibly dense. 'That doesn't matter at all; the new money doesn't count; it is *'asul*, your origins, that count and that is that.'

While I have been told by many women that not all families are so conscious of the importance of origins, those that I have observed have been. Some of the comments get downright nasty. 'Oh, well, she should be happy with him. She doesn't have a lot of choices, coming from her family.' Families who are not considered to be 'pure' Emirati can mean naturalized citizens or, as it is said, those 'given the passport,' such as Yemenis or Palestinians. Non-pure can also mean families who have Qatari, Saudi or Omani ancestors. *Ajami*, which means 'deaf to Arabic,' usually indicates those families who have Persian ancestors. Theoretically all non-Arabic speaking people are *Ajami*, but when an Emirati uses the word he/she means from Persia. Historically Persia was often called *ajam* in Arabic and the denotation has stuck. *Ajami*, I am told, are easily recognized because they have fairer skin, and this is often said with not a little jealousy. Fair skin is an important factor in reckoning beauty, and Emirati women avoid the sun like cats do water. *Ajami* is not always used pejoratively, but when coming from someone who considers herself to be 100 per cent Emirati it is definitely not complimentary. There are many very wealthy families who have a Persian or two in the family tree. Their wealth and success are not at issue, but when it comes to marriage their *Ajami* status might be a factor.

Children who have foreign mothers run a difficult gauntlet when it is time to marry. The level of difficulty is determined by the mother's background. Her background is not only considered ethnically but also includes whether or not she has converted to Islam; if she was not Muslim at the time of marriage; if she was a first wife; and her education level. Marriage for a young woman whose Indian mother is the not well educated second or third wife may be fraught with difficulty unless an arrangement is made with the son of a similarly situated young man. Sadly the same seems to hold true for those with Filipina mothers. Young Emiratis whose mothers are British, Irish and American face fewer difficulties, it appears, but I have been told that many families have been concerned that the marriage would not work out. I have pointed out that few Emirati marriages of any blend seem to 'work out' any more and so one naturally wonders why one sort of marriage is considered more at risk than others. The most frequent response is that mothers would worry about getting along with a daughter-in-law who, they automatically assume, would be more liberal or, failing that, just different.

I have had many students whose mothers are not Emirati, and quite a few have suffered through protracted and rather ugly divorces as their parents separated. Not only does their standard of living drop precipitously but their social status plummets as well. At the heart of the status drop is the fact that there is a widely held assumption that marriage is rather like employment sponsorship: once that contract is broken, the foreigner should return home. When the foreigner has lived in the country for twenty plus years and has children who are Emirati this is difficult for her to imagine, and even harder to enact. All of the divorce cases with which I have been involved peripherally through students and friends have been devastating to the wife and the children. In one such family the male children were unable to understand how their father could abandon them and took their anger and grief out on their mother. They imprisoned her in the home, ranted and raved at her incessantly, then finally drove her to the airport and, essentially, deported her. Their sisters didn't know what they had done for several days, and it was only weeks later that it was uncovered that their father had paid for the airline ticket. In another sad case, the girls of the family withdrew from university because they said they could not face questions from other students, or what they called negative attention. One student, Fatima, is half Indian and tells me that her life is difficult because of her mixed parentage. 'We have always had to walk a thin line as it is, being half something else.' Fatima's parents have divorced, and it has taken a toll on her university studies. She has gone to the family court several times to protest the fact that her father is not paying what is supposed to be mandatory upkeep for his children. 'It's like the whole world waits for us to stumble and fall. My mother always told me that I had to act in a way that no one could question ever, because people judge us more harshly.' Fatima's experience has been painful and unusual. One young woman whose mother is Filipina has a very different outlook. 'People may notice that I look a little different, but it has never made any difference to how they treat me. I am Emirati and that is that.' She is engaged now to a young man whose parents support their marriage fully and they have never mentioned her Filipina mother.

Other students say that they are little bothered by such things either. 'Emirati society is open. There are tons of families that have foreign-born mothers. It is accepted, after all it has to be because we are just as Emirati as someone whose mother was born in Oman or Qatar.' When we talk about who they will marry they see no difficulties. 'It won't be a problem. My parents are going to let me choose, so it will be a man that I know who knows me. I don't want to marry into some stuffy, super conservative family anyway.'

'Marrying up' for some women means marrying a *sheikh*, a man from the ruling families. For young *sheikhas*, the women of the ruling family, there is really only marriage within their extended family or marriage to a *sheikh* from one of the other emirates. Marrying into the ruling family has its pitfalls, not the least of which is constant observation and monitoring. The women of the ruling family have severe restrictions placed on their freedom of movement. There is too the fact that if divorced by a *sheikh* you probably won't be able to marry again—even though generally divorce carries no stigma, though this too seems to be changing. The young women of the ruling families whom I know, the *sheikhas*, seem rather resigned to the fact that sooner or later they will be told that their engagement has been arranged (if it is not already) and they will have little to say about it.

'What will become of them?'

Few young women want to be in the position of seriously considering becoming the second or third wife of an older man. Over the years only one has admitted to me that she would consider that as an option, but for her this would not be out of desperation but rather that she didn't really want to marry anyway and being the second or third wife might, in her mind, involve less pressure to have children and social obligations. For the other young women with whom I have discussed the possibility of being one of several wives, that is a fate worse than spinsterhood.

There are several families that say they have never had multiple wives and have no intention of starting now. First wives are rarely happy at the prospect of the husband taking another. They are even less happy when it is dumped in their lap as a fait accompli. I have watched two families unravel when the husband took another wife without informing his wife or his grown children that he intended to do so. In both cases the second wives were non-Emirati and much younger than the husband (and the first wife). In one of these families the first wife had a nervous breakdown and retired from public life altogether. In the other the wife decided to strike back and make the husband's life as difficult as possible, and, in fact, there was a rumor that she was considering finding someone who could cast spells against him and his new bride. Her friends, who told me the story, were completely horrified by this. They knew that she couldn't find someone to cast spells but they were appalled that she showed herself to be 'weak,' as they called it.

There are successful multiple-wife families too. They are few but I happen to know one family that is composed of four wives and dozens of children. Each mother and her children have a separate villa and lead separate lives in Abu Dhabi, but they vacation together as a group. Vacations apparently work so well that the wives insisted that the husband purchase an estate large enough to accommodate all of them in Switzerland.

6

BEING EMIRATI ISN'T EASY!

Emiratis, we are told by the media, are gravely concerned about their identity. The government of the UAE also makes frequent statements about the loss of Emirati identity and sponsors conferences at which the issue is discussed (El Shammaa 2009; Habboush 2009; Issa 2009). In the media several different types of identities are often conflated, so identity might be national in one instance and religious or cultural or both in the next. Of course, all of those identities are interconnected and self-referencing, and while all combine to make up an individual's identity, certain connotations will have more significance in some situations than others. Perhaps a telescope is an apt metaphor: the lens and the mechanism widen to encompass associations like 'fellow citizen' that are imagined, and narrow to exclude all but kin. It is the narrowest lens, that of family, that is most important to Emiratis. The wider view that includes all other citizens, i.e. national identity, was constructed in 1971; and while citizenship is guarded ferociously, Emiratis, especially in Abu Dhabi, remain closely identified with their home emirate.

There is a freshness and exuberance in Emiratis' recognition of their national identity, and indeed National Day celebrations across the country are festivals of flags and colors painted on faces, cars and buildings. To be a young country celebrating its third decade of existence is certainly grounds for pride; but to be young, incredibly wealthy and secure is cause for days of celebration each year.

Americans, who also like celebrating the Fourth of July with fire-works and flags, are put to shame by the frenzied activities in the UAE. During National Day celebrations, the Corniche along Abu Dhabi's waterfront is jammed with cars and pedestrians for several successive nights as fireworks light up the skies and music wafts up and down the road. The road itself is impassable by 8 p.m., and then car horns drown out the music and the roar of engines and squealing tires turns into a cacophony that drives even the bravest of us into retreat. The local newspapers typically include a selection of photos showing the traffic, the decorated cars, the painted faces and fireworks and then go on to bemoan the dangerous behavior of young men showing off, the number of small children seen hanging dangerously from sunroofs and the chaos of the celebration. At the university, students decorate the campus in the colors of the flag, gently but persuasively insist that the whole faculty should try wearing national dress, and organize an evening of celebration that is never actually on the day itself because on that day most of the students want to be a part of the public celebrations on the streets of the city.

I capitalize on these performances of national identity every year with readings and discussions about the social construction of national identity and the related topics of patriotism and national-ism. The students groan loudly and piteously as they slog their way through at least some of the selections assigned in *Imagined Communities*, *Banal Nationalism* and *Ethnicity and Nationalism* and wrestle with the concepts of citizen, ethnicity, ethnocentrism, homogeneity and heterogeneity (Anderson 1983; Billig 1995; Erik-sen 2002). The discussions that follow are intriguing, and though these students are not a random sample by any means, they are an indication of how age twenty—something Emirati women think about these issues and highlight those factors that are perceived threats to Emirati identity.

The word Emirati is as new as the country. It is a *nisbah* adjec-tive formed from *emarat*, the Arabic plural in United Arab Emir-ates. The equivalent in the United States would be to call Americans 'Stateys.' Up until the federation of the seven individually ruled emirates, there was little need for identification outside of the family and tribe. In cases of travel, such as to Makah for the pilgrimage or for trade, if tribe was not sufficient, then the ruler's name or the name of the largest town would be used. One still hears Emiratis refer to Abu Dhabi as dar Zayed, which translates roughly as the locality or abode of Sheikh Zayed. Many Emiratis call themselves 'locals' and often indicate other Emiratis that way too, and it is not uncommon to hear sentences such as 'they have to hire more locals' or 'was it a local who did that?' When speaking in Arabic the word used is *muwatin*, native, from the trilateral root *wa-ta-na*, from which homeland, national and indigenous are also formed. In most languages and in most countries, a linguistic distinction is made between native-born and not, citizen and not, though the referent might be village rather than nation or predating incursion and settlement by others as in the 'first' of Canada's indigenous population. In the Emirates several distinctions are made. The basis for all of the distinctions is that of citizenship or, as it more commonly referred to, 'having the passport.' Citizenship in this wealthy country connotes benefits such as healthcare, government houses, education, pensions, social welfare, subsidized electricity and water, and access to other resources such as cash to spend on a wedding, agricultural land, and the ability to sponsor foreign workers (*kafeel*). Citizenship in the UAE is economically beneficial, and that is why 'getting the passport' is such an emotionally charged statement. In earlier years citizenship was awarded quite freely, especially here in Abu Dhabi where Sheikh Zayed granted passports to men (and their families) in recognition of their work in building the country. The majority of these new citizens were Arabs from other countries—Palestinians, Yemenis and Egyptians. Some adopted new names for their passports like Ahmad, a Yemeni who had fled from his home when the Marxists took over, and, after a brief stay in Kuwait, landed in Abu Dhabi. When he was given citizenship he took the name 'al Harbi,' the warrior, as much to have a name that sounded tribal as anything else.

Ahmad was smart to make up his new name rather than, as others have done, to pick a family name already in use. The only name that is sacrosanct in Abu Dhabi is al Nahayan, the name of the ruling family. All others seem to be fair game, and this is more than a little irritating to the families already in possession of those names. I stumbled into this emotional firestorm one day when I told an acquaintance that I had just been introduced to someone from his family. When I gave him the full name of the person he turned red and blurted out angrily that the man I had met was a fake, a liar and worse. 'He's not even Emirati!!' he hissed. 'He's half Omani and half something else!' Fadel was furious. 'Why do they let them do that?'

Another family whose name has been appropriated by others whom they know about has taken to referring to them as *'faux'* and they take great pains to correct any presumptions that the counterfeits are related in any manner. In tribal societies one's name is more than a name, it is an affiliation, it is honor, and it is everything. In the US few people would make the assumption that all 'Smiths' are related excepted in a dim and distant past; but in the UAE, the last name, the tribal name, does still carry the presumption of kin. When that presumption is coupled with the fact that the Emirati community in Abu Dhabi is relatively small, the result is that people also assume that all al Mansouris know each other. In conversation Emiratis usually quickly establish tribal group and then family, the branch of the tribe. I spoke to one woman who was very upset when a friend had asked her if she had a cousin working in a particular office because someone with her name had been fired. Meera was exasperated and worried at the same time. 'We have no control over these people who take our names! Do we know where they live? Do we know how they behave? No, they are strangers to us, but now they carry our name and so what they do can ultimately bring shame on us if the truth is not known. And now it is on my head to explain that this thief is not of my family! Why, oh why was it our name that she used?'

Deeper than the dismay and perhaps dishonor that taking names may cause is the distinction made on the basis of one's family being 'pure Emirati.' Though the connotation made is to bloodlines, in actuality the denotation is the length of time that a family has been settled here and, importantly, how long they have been considered to be a *muwatin*. This is a very prickly subject and in class it can cause discomfort for the students. Normally only those who consider themselves to be 'pure' ever use the word or make references to it. In class students who are about to talk about pure Emiratis typically look around the room first to determine who might be offended. All of the conversations I have had with students about this issue have been outside of class; I learned quickly to steer away and keep discussions safely off this quicksand.

'It's the families that have lived here for generations, like my family. We need to separate ourselves from those who came later.' Why, I ask? 'Well, it's complicated but it is important that we know who we are and that we have a higher status than the others.' I jokingly point out that historically all Arabs originated in the Yemen and so everyone is ultimately a Yemeni transplant; my comment provokes anger: 'Yes, but that was a long time ago, before nations and states; now it is Yemenis who have a nation.' That comment is telling, because when I have heard other Emiratis talk about this topic, they too point out that their ancestors were here long before it was a nation-state, long before oil was discovered and, in their mind, long before it was economically beneficial to become an Emirati. They talk about the families who were here two hundred years ago, who suffered and lived hard lives. There is a sense of endowment in these arguments; a belief that only those who lived through the bad times should be able to enjoy the benefits of oil. My student, Amna, expresses that sentiment clearly. 'The families who should have it easy now are the families that were here, like mine! Why should those people who came after oil benefit from what we have here?' I remind her that her family left for a while when they could not pay their debts and hid in Qatari territory. 'But the point is that we were here to do that!' End of that conversation.

For some Emiratis, endowment is not the key to understanding current discussions of 'purity.' Some people interpret the discussion as another form of competition. 'Purity and who is a "real Emirati" is all about money and prestige. We have so much money floating around that we have to find something else to compete about and now it has come down to prestige—that is one thing that money really can't buy!' We are talking about origins, purity and access to power. The last is a tricky subject to broach with anyone—more dangerous to ask those who have access to power, and much more informative to ask those who do not. I am talking to a man who does by virtue of his family's long-standing connections to and support of the ruling family. Khalid does not appear to be defensive about the topic and so we continue. 'I know that there are tribal groups, parts of certain tribes that think they haven't gotten their fair share, but the truth of the matter is much more complicated than it seems. It isn't as easy as dividing the pie into equal parts—some people, some families, earned their share by hard work, by supporting the rulers' decisions, by becoming part of the new system. Others just sat back and did nothing and now complain that they have been "left out."' Khalid sits back in his chair and laces his fingers together, thinking. 'Of course it is easier for me because I have the name that I have, but why shouldn't I reap the rewards of my great grandfather's bravery, my grandfather's work, and my father's position? Why not, I ask?' I ask how he thinks that other Emiratis feel about his good fortune. 'They are angry, but they know there is nothing they can really do—this is not a meritocracy, after all; it is tribal, and that is how things work.'

I call this tribal modern, and it is contentious. Sheikh Zayed as President and Sheikh Khalifa as Crown Prince and ruler of Abu Dhabi worked to ensure that the benefits of oil permeated down to all the people, and they were successful to a degree. However, the governments—federal and emirate—reflect tribal loyalties that precede oil, and to this day access to what Emiratis often call 'the real money' is largely granted on personal, family ties. This is not to say that the rest of the population has been ignored, far from it. The list of benefits, starting with no taxes of any sort, is enough to make the citizens of the UK and USA extremely jealous. But excellent salaries, pensions, free education and healthcare lose their luster when confronted with private airplanes, multiple palaces, million dollar license plates, and other excesses that are public; the private excesses are best not mentioned.

Khalid is right, this is not a meritocracy, but not all status is ascribed: hard work does achieve; but it appears that for some, work doesn't get you far enough. Some Emiratis I have interviewed have been very successful and claim that the sky is the limit if you work hard. One of my former students has risen high and fast and now is called 'Her Excellency' and all without the family connections that are often assumed to be more important than merit. In addition to family (and tribal) connections, the ability to mobilize *waasta* is often seen as a way to circumvent channels to get a good job, solve problems and gain access to those with power. *Waasta* means to mediate, to act as a go-between and to act on someone's behalf. *Waasta* is misunderstood and consequently misused by the expatriate community, in which it is a synonym for power. In reality, those who have power don't need *waasta* because they don't need someone to act on their behalf or to approach a powerful person with their petition. *Waasta* is better understood as having connections to people who have better connections.

As with notions of 'pureness,' *waasta* is rarely mentioned by those Emiratis who have it, and those who don't claim that the abuse of *waasta* is crippling the country. 'It is corruption really! How can some stupid person who never studied anything suddenly be given a great salary while my brother sits at home watching dust settle on his degree?' It does no good to argue that we cannot know the qualifications of every person, that it is just as possible for an al Za'abi or al Mansouri to be highly qualified and capable; I am told that is not the point. 'People who have good *waasta* get all the good chances, no matter what, and that isn't fair.' Fairness and equality are issues that are brought up for discussion in classes more and more frequently.

The stratifications, the divisions within Emirati society are deep, and yet visually Emirati society is homogeneous. This is often confusing for expatriates who assume that all Emiratis are equally wealthy, equally high ranking and equally empowered. In good measure the veneer of homogeneity is accomplished by the nearly universal adoption of national dress. Women wear the *'abayah*, a floor-length black over-dress, and *shaylah*, a headscarf worn to cover the hair and neckline that is by and large black but usually adorned with embroidery or other decorative effect. Men wear a crisp-looking white *kandoura*, a full-length tailored garment, along with the *agaal* and *gutra*, the headcloth and black rope that secures it on the head. I have been told that the genesis of the distinctive black and white national dress, common throughout the Gulf, was first adopted as a means of making the indigenous population distinct from the foreigners now living in their midst. Supposedly this was also to help Emiratis recognize each other because there were many Arabs from other countries like Egypt, Lebanon, Jordan and Syria who might have been mistakenly identified. I have not been able to document this narrative but most of the older women with whom I have discussed this agree. They find it rather amusing when their grandchildren refer to 'national dress' as traditional clothing because, they say, there was no possible way that a white *kandoura* would have been worn regularly before there was running water, washing machines, irons, starch and, to be honest, maids. A glimpse at any of the pictures taken of people before the late 1960s shows men dressed in various shades of brown and black, and not white. Only the rulers seem to have managed white with any frequency. The *'abayah* was worn in the pre-oil days but, as one woman pointed out, you were never really in the 'public view' in the settlements and towns so it did not have to be worn all the time.

'It isn't national dress any more, it's the national uniform,' laughs Masifa. 'It is the only way we can be recognized as citizens.' She is right: Emiratis in their national uniform are immediately identifiable on the streets of the city and in the malls. Not only recognized as Emirati, but for most expatriates the next assumption is that they will demand privileged service, access or priority. When I point this out to students they get angry. 'But that is crap! We get treated worse than you do in the shops.' 'Oh really? How is it then that I am frequently ignored in shops when an Emirati woman enters? And why do the attendants at the petrol station run to a car with black windows when there are others who were waiting longer?' I wait to be told once again that my experiences are aberrations, that really Emiratis are treated badly; I have had this discussion a hundred times before. 'They raise the prices for us because they think we have more money.' 'You honestly think that prices are raised?' Class after class of students does think that prices quoted to Emiratis are higher.

So, I ask, why then wear a black *'abayah*? Why dress to be immediately identified as an Emirati? Silence, and then from a very thoughtful and usually quiet student in the back: 'We expect all to be treated like princesses.' Yes, I say. 'Perhaps because we think that even if we can't push each other around, we can push you foreigners around—that makes us feel more powerful. None of us feels like we have any other power, even the men.' I am more than a little stunned with this honesty and hope that the other students will pursue the many issues she has raised. It takes two more class sessions before other students are prepared to voice their opinions. 'It isn't easy being Emirati; it seems that we are disliked because we have money, made fun of because we are lazy, laughed at because we like to buy designer labels and I think most people want us to fail.' There is an element of truth in everything Shamma has said. 'No matter what we do, how we dress, how we behave, where we go, who we talk to or don't talk to, what we buy, what kind of car we drive—there are negative comments, we aren't doing it "right" by someone else's standards.'

Being judged by others' standards is a comment made frequently by Emiratis, both in classes and in discussions elsewhere. I have talked with many women who express the opinion that they have more money than 'taste' or style. Women tell me they worry that they really don't know how to choose the right furniture, dishes, carpets and other furnishings for their houses and so they just buy the most expensive, partially convinced that if it costs a lot it must be good. I had a bizarre conversation at an embassy reception one night with an expatriate woman who was an interior designer. 'It is the easiest job in Abu Dhabi!' she assured me with a broad smile. 'They [meaning Emirati women] come to me and say "do my house," and so I draw up designs using the most expensive brocades, Italian marble, enormous crystal chandeliers, silk carpets, canopied beds, lacquered dressers, then add pillars and columns and half a dozen huge sofas and I am done. No one ever disputes my design and no one ever says "how much?"' I ask her if she is proud of the designs she is creating for people. 'Pride has nothing to do with it; no one sees these designs—only other Emirati women will see them and if they like what they see they will call me too. I don't create these designs for my portfolio; this is a money factory here.'

Three months later I was led around a friend's house to see the wonderful changes that had been made during a 'renovation' that

113

had taken six months of construction. It was hard to know what to say when confronted with mirrors and marble, sofas the size of aircraft carriers, stylized lamps and silk plants and heavy brocade draperies. The glossy black and white squares on the floor were art deco; the walls were surely 'orientalist' and the remainder was somewhere between baroque and burlesque. I was speechless. She was happy with the result but still seemed less than satisfied. 'It isn't exactly what I expected,' she said somewhat tentatively. 'I didn't think it would be so, what's the word? Busy?' I asked if she had given the designer instructions. 'Oh no, we never do, it is useless as they do what they want anyway, and besides, I wouldn't know what to tell her.' I sat on one of the new sofas. It was unbelievably uncomfortable. 'I am surprised at the new bathroom down here,' I said. The usual Emirati guest bathroom has at least three sinks and a private toilet. The multiple sinks are necessary for all guests to wash before prayers and to clean fingers after eating (especially when eating 'traditional' style without cutlery). 'Yes,' my friend mused. 'That is going to take some getting used to, but we were told that it is the new style to have a compact bathroom so we said yes.' The new bathroom was indeed compact and very stylized with ultra-modern fixtures, black tiles with a copper hue on the floors and walls and one tiny sink. 'Where will you put all the colognes and perfumes?' Every bathroom I have visited had a wonderful array of both, plus usually ornate boxes containing tissues, hair combs, hand *crèmes* and a generous choice of soaps. 'I guess we don't need them any more,' she replied. When visiting again the next week, I was not at all surprised to see that a little black lacquered table had been installed in the bathroom and held a collection of perfumes.

I remembered my first visit to an Emirati home in 2001 when I had been so impressed that I had remarked upon the number of bathrooms. 'Of course we have so many bathrooms! We have in this villa nine bathrooms.' Her smile was wide. 'When you come from the desert as we have, there can never be too many bathrooms or too much water.' Ayesha had, in a very personal way, put her finger on the dichotomous quality inherent in being an Emirati; life was difficult in the past, and while Emiratis want to keep the memory of their history, keep traditions alive, most work hard to distance themselves from the poverty and the harshness.

Of course, it isn't just about water or bathrooms or the size and opulence of new villas, roads and malls. Those are the material barriers that keep the memory of poverty at a distance. The material barriers are substantial and seemingly incontrovertible in the shape of roads, walls and buildings that mark the desert border of the cities. Emiratis also construct narratives that sever ties with the impoverished past by focusing on their new identity as established, urban, cosmopolitan people with villas, cars and servants. These narrative barriers are also substantial but they are dynamic and fluid and are reframed according to the social situation. My students need no such narrative for they have no memory of poverty at all. Their grandmothers do remember and they talk about their earlier lives in vivid detail. It is their mothers who may remember the first medical doctors to arrive in the emirate, or the opening of the Abu Dhabi airport, but they have no recollection of want; they remember roads under construction, new buildings going up, new shops replacing *suqs*, schools and universities opening and a constantly changing life.

'We have never had a present, not at least since oil; it has all been future for us. What shall we build? What shall we develop now? We plant trees in the desert and called it reforestation—that is a joke; there were no forests there, not in any of our memories at least! We have built modern cities, tree-lined highways and some of the biggest shopping malls in the world. Are we happy? Are we finished? No. We look around to see what else can be built, what can be expanded, what will tell the world who we are. We don't just build, you see, we make statements.' Making statements is something that Emiratis have done well. Largest, tallest, most expensive, seven star, the world's only are all Emirati statements. Granted, most are in Dubai but Abu Dhabi is gaining ground in the race to have world-class everything. Dubai boasts the man-made islands of Palm, Jumeirah and Jebel Ali, the Burj al Dubai that will be the tallest building, Dubailand, a Disneyland-like part that will, of course, dwarf all competitors. Emiratis—at least those planning and funding such mega-developments—see no limits to what they

115

can do, and that is, unfortunately, behavior that encourages the stereotypical image of rich show-offs whose wealth has allowed them to refashion their world and themselves.

Arabs from other countries who live here often refer to Emiratis as coarse cousins who have no appreciation of anything that does not glitter; they belittle them and say they are upstarts and sham artists. 'They have no idea what they're doing!' says one Egyptian who has lived and worked here for years. 'They travel outside the country, see something that they like and then come home and have it built. No understanding, no plan for what they're doing—the country looks like a child's room with toys strewn all over the floor.' His words are harsh but familiar because they reflect the envy and resentment expressed frequently, albeit in private.

Yet, there is a bit of truth to such comments. In the rush to create the future, the Emiratis have built and built. Abu Dhabi Island is being enlarged, again. Truckload after truckload of sand was dumped in the shallow waters to add enough 'land' to build a bigger Corniche. Dubai has grown to meet Jebel Ali on the one end and Sharjah on the other. Is the economy supporting this growth? No, say many Emiratis and foreigners working with the inadequate and mostly unreliable data that are available, not in real terms. It is oil revenue controlled by the rulers that is being spent—money that many argue should be invested in education, training, R&D and, most importantly, spent on developing a sustainable economy—not one that is dependent on the extraction and export of the one and only natural resource and not one dependent on foreigners. They have built a future that is not supported by their present. The 'Crossroads of the World' character of Dubai, with its Global Village and new 'innovation zones' like Knowledge Village and Media City, heralds a bright and shining future. The reality is that there are not enough educated and trained Emiratis yet to fill the buildings—the national population is not large enough to maintain the economy of the country. It is foreigners who are building the future here and some Emiratis wonder where they fit in that future.

While criticising and denigrating Emiratis seems to be almost an indoor sport when expatriates compete against each other with stories about Emirati behavior, it is the criticism that Emiratis level at themselves that is more important. This criticism is much more intense and reveals their fear and doubts. Emiratis have worked hard to create a world for themselves, a world of comfort that was unthinkable fifty years ago. Their fear is that they may have out-stripped their ability to manage the world they have built. There is an undercurrent of doubt about what they are doing and how they are doing it. Emiratis doubt their ability to judge their successes and failures. Western consultants come and go with new ideas, new models, new ways to measure success, and new best practices only to leave in their wake reports and recommendations most of which are not implemented and gather dust until the next consultants arrive to suggest another new model. Something always needs to be changed; the present is not allowed to mature, ideas do not ripen. New programs are needed, new catch phrases, new techniques, new anything and everything that will create the future that is coming. 'What we have is just not good enough,' Hamad tells me. 'We are never content, it seems; we will do something else, begin again, start from scratch because the future is there, just in front of us, and even though we are moving toward it, it is out of reach.'

This non-present of the Emiratis is supported in part by ignoring the past. Emiratis are intensely proud of their Bedouin tradition of hospitality and honor and the ethos of self-reliance that it repre-sents to them. There are several government institutions whose missions are to promote the preservation of the traditions of camel racing, poetry, falconry and dhow building. His Highness Sheikh Zayed was very vocal about the need to preserve the past, and his statement that a people without a past has no future is quoted widely and yet it is just as widely misunderstood. Traditions and heritage are important, but they do not add up to history. They are snapshots taken in time, or rather, taken out of time. They are mementos, snapshots of the techniques and skills that give us a glimpse into a way of life when falconry was used to augment a rather meager diet. Taken out of context, separated from the socio-cultural milieu that supported them, such things are trivialized and have become entertaining hobbies to enjoy on elaborately choreo-graphed trips into the desert where permanent tents and domestic servants await the arrival of caravans of 4x4s. Indigenous architecture, assiduously avoided in the building of the modem cities, now lends itself to creating heritage tourist attractions, so wind towers adorn restaurants and modern interpretations of Arabian tents define the roofs of shopping malls.

These snapshots from the past are everywhere, it seems, leading one to think that the Emiratis are not only proud of their past but wish to be constantly reminded of it. In most contexts, however, the pictures of the past are simply decorations, wall coverings in corporate offices. Old black and white photographs taken before the discovery of oil with banged up Land Rovers, young men with the wild long hair of the desert and sandy tracks around *'arish* (palm frond) huts hang on the granite, marble and ultra-modern chrome walls that define the new Emirati society. The pictures are interesting but they hang without explanation and it isn't long before you realize that it is the same set of pictures that are repeated, building after building. I have asked but have not found any young Emirati who can tell me more than the obvious fact that the pictures are old. They look at them and shake their heads. 'Don't know where that is, must be Abu Dhabi. Don't know who the men are but they must be sheikhs if they are hanging in here.'

For the younger generation of Emiratis the past—their past—is alien to them in a way more dramatic than the usual gap between generations. My parents told me tales of farm life and walking miles through blizzards to get to school, the North American version of the stories older family members tell to instill in the young an appreciation of the past and the values that went with it. In most societies parents and grandparents are able to convey a sense of continuity when they tell these stories. Life has gotten better now and easier with the technology that has transformed how we live. The farms still exist, you can see the old farmhouse, the schools are old and battered and in some cases replaced by huge complexes, but they are, for the most part, still there to look at. My parents' first house might have been small and cramped but there it was and I could connect the images in my mind, creating at least a rough sense of them and that time grows, that the past merges with the present and the future. For Emiratis it is difficult to create such a sense of continuity, of the present arising from the past, because when a young Emirati looks out on where his or her grandparents lived there is nothing to see—it has been transformed into something that has no connection with the land or the past.

This is not because there is no past here. The archaeological record of the area shows that people have lived in this part of the Arabian peninsula for at least 5,000 years and recent finds suggest that this may go back as far as 7,000 years. Artifacts found in Tel Abrak, between Sharjah and Ajman, suggest that there was established trade with the Indus Valley and Ur by 2,000 BCE. The past is there and its record is growing as archaeologists work to complete the picture of settlements, trade and the movement of peoples over thousands of years. This past, the far past, is ignored by all but a few Emiratis.

It seems that for most that past is thought to be just another part of the pre-Islamic time of ignorance, *jahiliyya. Jahiliyya* is worse than remote and meaningless, it is dangerous because it was the time before revelation and peopled by unbelievers and pagans. The past has nothing to give us and can teach us nothing because it has no connection to the Muslim worldview. That past, *jahiliyya* all of it, is as disconnected as is the idea of life on Mars. That was a time that had to end because it was to be superseded by revelation, knowledge and the birth of the community of believers who should not look back to ignorance.

Rejecting history includes more than *jahiliyya* times, and it seems that anything that does not bear directly on the immediate is of no interest and of questionable value. Soon after arriving in the country, I was teaching a course in anthropology and talking about the importance of historical perspective. I went on for a while, trying to keep my momentum, undaunted in front of a sea of uninterested faces. Then I stopped and asked them questions about what they knew of history. For the students in that classroom and all the students who have followed them, there are but three historical periods. There is the pre-Islamic past, *jahiliyya*; the Islamic period; and then Sheikh Zayed. The first for them is an unknown, a black hole with no facts or features to distinguish any of the millennia within it. The Prophet Muhammad and the rise and spread of Islam are of course a part of religious identity. But when I asked specific questions about, for example, the Companions of the Prophet, the construction of the first mosque at Medina or the collection of Hadith, a few of the students said that they had not studied the actual history of Islam.

Then the third historical period is Sheikh Zayed and oil. There is some confusion about whether or not oil preceded Sheikh Zayed since he has become synonymous with wealth and prosperity for most Emiratis. My students had very little knowledge about the colonial period when the British called the area the Trucial States, or the role they played in legitimizing the rule of the royal families in each of the seven Emirates. No, for these university students, the country and life begin with Sheikh Zayed and they titter and giggle when looking at old pictures that illustrate a very different time in their own country. 'Who are these people?' I asked them. Many of them, I knew, especially those from prominent Abu Dhabi families, were looking at their grandfathers but they had no inkling that there was any connection between themselves and the photos.

This is more significant than not being taught, or as is the case often with young adults, just not caring about anything that happened in the past and dismissing everything from the time of black and white. This is historical disconnect. Young Emiratis seem to look at their pre-oil history in the same way they regard the *jahili-yya* time before the Prophet: a black hole devoid of meaning and relevance. It is hard to find no meaning in a past that bears no connection with their present and even less with the future they are creating. More significant perhaps than their inability to recognize grandfathers in the pictures is their inability to recognize the connection to themselves. This sense of disconnect may well be one of the effects of the massive, rapid and indeed breathtaking development over the past forty years. In two generations the Emiratis have built a remarkable country. They have also built an edifice that protects them not only from the harsh desert but also—and perhaps more importantly—from the memory of a trying and impoverished past.

This barrier, this separation from the desert and history, tends to hide origins and allows a new and better reality to take its place. Simple plain houses are enlarged and remodeled and suddenly the past looks more like it should, more like the present. The original houses of the ruler at Al Ain are lost within the new complex built around the area and visitors are encouraged to believe that this is as it was in the past, just 'cleaned up a bit.' This reconstruction of reality is not confined to the historic buildings; it permeates society. One day when I was expressing my frustration with a history class, my Emirati friends summed up what they thought was the essence of the problem. 'We love our heritage but we don't like to be reminded that we were poor! We like to think that we have always lived in spacious villas; we have always had luxury cars and the roads on which to drive. We forget that sometimes people went hungry and that our grandparents were often in debt to the pearl merchants. We don't like to remember that our babies died because we didn't have any doctors. We have a new life now and we have a new story.' As we discussed their new story, the new narrative, we talked about what happens when the new story clashes with the old, as it still does.

Large social events bring many people together, and at such events there is the potential for the old and new stories to collide with one another. This is especially true at weddings, because most families will not yet flaunt the time-honored Bedouin tradition of inviting all to the wedding of their children. Distant relations, acquaintances and even strangers can join the celebration. All they have to do is arrive at the villa gate or hotel lobby. I have attended several weddings over the past years—the women's side of the fes-tivities. With only one exception, at each of the weddings unantici-pated guests arrived and seemed to upset the tone and atmosphere of the party. It was readily apparent that they were, in a sense, interlopers from another story, an older reality, from the past. In all these cases the interlopers were older women, who wore rather simple unadorned 'abayahs and, I was told, old-style burqahs. They seemed a bit foreign to the lavish surroundings and stood in sharp contrast to the other guests with coifed hair and designer gowns bought in Beirut and London. They were politely greeted and wel-comed but they did not sit down to chat or socialize with anyone. In only one case was it clear that the one woman who had arrived was related to the bride's family. These women had come to eat and to carry away with them what food they could carry. They set upon the platters of lamb and baby goat, the mountains of rice and exquisitely wrapped and displayed Belgian chocolates with single-mindedness. They were not rude, they were not ill-behaved; they had come to eat and that is what they did. The other guests moved away as best they could from the buffet tables and watched. It was hard to tell if they were making space for the unexpected guests or if they were trying to dissociate themselves from those guests and what they were doing. At five of the weddings the mother of the bride sought me out immediately and began to apologize by way of explanation. The words of the apology varied little. The women were from the desert, they didn't live in the city, they don't know how to behave at these sorts of things, and they will be gone soon. All wanted my assurance that I wasn't upset by their appearance and that I understood that the women were not like them.

The old women reveal the flaw in the fabric that these families have so carefully woven and their presence disturbed the party, more so perhaps with the additional factor of me as a witness. The new story and the old story do not easily share the same space—the differences are too great. And the new story is too new, too fragile, and too thin to survive when juxtaposed with reminders of the past that is being forgotten systematically. The official guests at all the weddings acted as if they had been invaded, violated by the appearance of the older women. The new story lives in the city, it was built along with the beautiful villas and their manicured gardens, brocade draperies, marble floors, maids and cooks. When that safe, comfortable new environment is breached by living, breathing reminders of how things were—that a wedding feast fed everyone and redistributed wealth, reinforcing alliances and bonds—the new story collapses.

Away from Abu Dhabi in smaller towns the stories seem to coexist more easily and sometimes the old story dominates. A wedding I attended in Al Ain was less opulent and formal, yet there were many more people and much more food. The party seemed, at least to me, to be more of a family gathering, a reunion rather than a social event. There seemed to be no one who was not expected and certainly no one who was not really wanted. Old women arrived, supported in some cases by their daughters and granddaughters, and all were greeted with great respect. They were given seats of honor and the younger women took the time to sit and talk with them in what was a rather involved receiving line. They were served from the buffet and constantly attended so that they didn't have to leave their prominent seats. Then, before the live music was scheduled to start, they were encouraged to talk, to tell stories. They looked at each other and looked at us. 'Stories? You want to hear stories?' Then they began and for the time that they talked, taking turns, interrupting each other, adding details and contradicting each other, the other guests were enthralled. They talked about the old life, the closeness of people, the ties that bound families together, the good times when the date harvest was rich and the bad times when the price of pearls stared to drop and the men stayed in debt from one season to the next. They told stories about the bride's mother and how the commotion caused by a very pregnant camel in distress had interrupted her wedding. They told funny stories, memories that made them laugh at themselves. They told sad stories, memories that made us all silent. They talked about the power they had in the old days, reminding the younger women that it was the wives and mothers who controlled the purse strings when they had so little, and that women had the freedom they had to visit relatives and friends. They bemoaned the new life that had separated them from their memories. 'In the old days, it was better because we were together, we knew each other and we knew ourselves. Now we are strangers in our own land, surrounded by foreigners, letting them tend to our children, and we are prisoners behind the pretty walls of the villas.'

I was impressed by their stories and by the sentiments that they were expressing. It was even more fascinating to watch the younger women react to the stories, nodding their heads as if in agreement. These were the old stories; the living memories of the past and the younger generation were listening attentively—this was something I had not seen before. The women continued to talk for another half an hour and then they seemed to tire as one and abruptly announced that they should leave, that they were old and needed to be in their beds soon. They rose from their seats and began saying

123

their goodbyes, kissing four and five times on one cheek in the Emirati style. One approached me and asked if I had understood their stories. Yes, I replied, I had understood and had enjoyed them all. I told her that I had not heard these stories, that the stories I had been told in Abu Dhabi were quite different. '*Akeed*,' she said, of course! 'Abu Dhabi stories are bought from the shops now; they are all new and clean and tell tales of a people that I don't know!'

For those who remember and tell the old stories, I am sure that the new story is just that: something else bought in a shop right along with everything else that fills people's homes and lives. They are the new truths. These are the truths that protect people from questioning, protect them from the fear that all they now enjoy is a phantom, a mirage that can disappear as quickly as it came. As one of my Emirati colleagues said one day when we were discussing the future, 'We like to tell ourselves that we earned all this, but we didn't, and I am afraid that we have squandered much of it. What will happen if the oil and the money dry up? We don't know how to live in this land any more.'

7

TRADITIONS AND THE FUTURE

Concern that exposure to the different cultural traditions brought into the UAE by foreigners and those broadcast into homes via satellite channels will ultimately result in a devaluation of Emirati ways is very real, but such worries are perhaps over-stated in the media. There is a greatly renewed public interest in poetry, and several competitions award poets handsomely. There are too associations in each emirate that support traditional folkdance, story-telling and intangible heritage.

Some traditions are fading as the older generation passes away. The *burqah*, the distinctive face mask worn by Emirati women, is worn by fewer and fewer women. The origins of the *burqah* are a little fuzzy. Soffan (1980) indicates a centuries-old Indian origin that makes it arguably non-Islamic. Others think that the *burqah* originated in either the Yemen or Oman, but it is impossible to verify. In the territory of the Emirates, the *burqah* was worn by both *badu wa hadr*, Bedouin and settled women. The deep dye, stiff material and rock-polished finish of the cloth *burqah* make it look almost metallic. Women who have worn the *burqah* since they were married and would never think of taking it off except to pray have discovered that it draws too much attention in Europe because people think that it is made of gold! The *burqah* stays on until the plane is landing in London and then a switch is made to the black fabric veil called *niqab*.

Investigating the origins of the *burqah* was a great excuse to talk about it. Alyazia wears one to every wedding, but when I asked her where the tradition of wearing the *burqah* came from, she was stumped. 'I have no idea where it came from. All I know is that when I was getting married they told me to put it on.' I was told a similar story by just about everyone I asked. A few said they had started to wear it when they had reached puberty but they added that 'for most it starts with marriage.' The origins of the *burqah* itself might be lost but not so an Emirati tradition associated with it; if wearing the *burqah* started with your marriage then you must wear a *burqah* to all weddings. Many women wear the *burqah* now only at weddings. This was confusing when my acquaintances suddenly appeared all wearing *burqahs*. I couldn't recognize anyone! Worse still, as we entered the banquet hall where the wedding celebration was taking place, fully half of the women there were also wearing a *burqah*. I followed shoes and handbags as they at least were identifiable—to my untrained eye, everyone looked pretty much identical. My friends thought this was hysterically funny and even more fun to imitate each other's voices to see if they could really trick me. I prayed for a fast learning curve as I focused in on eyes, eyebrows and mouths.

There are many different *burqah* styles. All are meant to reproduce the features of the *saqr*, the falcon, a symbol of grace, pride and strength. The eye slits are cut first; then the edges are finished and a seam is sewn to form a sleeve in the middle. In that center sleeve is inserted a stick, called *saif*, meaning sword, that keeps the front straight. Smaller pieces of *saif* are sewn in the top corner folds to keep it somewhat rigid. *Shubug* are the strings used to tie the *burqah* around the head. The material used is saturated with dye, and strategically placed masking tape prevents the dye from staining the face in the sweltering heat and humidity of Abu Dhabi. Named styles, or cuts, include the Dubai style, also called Za'beel, with a thin top and broad curved bottom; and Al Ain design, which is thin on both the top and bottom. Other designs are squarer like those from Qatar, and the ones from Oman are larger with the top rising up on the forehead.

The width and breadth of the *burqah* vary from style to style. The width also varies with the age of the woman wearing it. As women age, the *burqah* they wear gets a little wider with the pass-ing years. I asked my friends about this and they laughed. 'Oh yes, you see it isn't just modesty that makes us wear the *burqah*! It has a functional purpose too: it hides the wrinkles!' Younger women normally wear a *burqah* that is quite narrow; in fact, narrower than the face of the person wearing it and just deep enough to cover the top of the mouth. Older women wear wide *burqahs* that completely cover the sides of the face, and theirs are longer, cover-ing the mouth completely.

'I have always thought that my mother is more beautiful when she is wearing the *burqah*. Don't you?' I had to admit that I didn't, but, over the course of several years and many weddings, I have gotten accustomed to the *burqah* and can recognize my friends. In my eyes it doesn't make them more beautiful individually, but I do think that it gives them an air of confident authority and power.

The *burqah* may be slowly fading away, but the traditional cel-ebrations of Ramadan, the feasts of Eid al Fitr and Eid al Adha, and the value and importance given to both hospitality and gener-osity are alive and well in Abu Dhabi. The holy month of Ramadan is honored as well as celebrated. It is of course a month set aside for fasting, contemplation and studying the Quran. In Abu Dhabi, Ramadan is a celebration of family and home. It is also occasion to wear traditional clothes and to eat traditional Emirati foods. Dur-ing the month of Ramadan I observe in class more *serwal*, baggy pants tightened around the ankle that are worn under long dresses, *jalabba*, than I see over the course of the other eleven months of the year. Ramadan, say most of my students, draws them back to their roots, and therefore they wear traditional clothes and eat tradi-tional foods. During the rest of the year it seems only the presence of grandma in the house can force some of these young women out of their jeans and into a loosely cut *jalabba*.

Offices, schools and businesses close during the afternoon during Ramadan to give people time to rest and prepare the foods that will be served later when the day's fast is broken. The fast is broken at home with family, whenever possible, and woe to those who are on the streets during the half an hour before the fast ends because peo-ple literally race to get home in time. Among the American expatriate community this is jokingly called the 'Ramadan 500' and no one wants to be caught up in it. The fast is broken first with a little water, a thin yoghurt-like drink called *laban*, or blackcurrant Ribena and some dates, in the manner of the Prophet Muhammad, and sustained here as a cherished tradition and a reminder of past days when oftentimes only dates were plentiful. Then it is prayer for the adults and teenagers who have been fasting while the little kids wait patiently (or not). The family reunites to eat in about 10 minutes. In many homes the meal is eaten in the kitchen, on the floor sitting on a thick carpet with pillows and bolsters to lean against. Other families arrange the food on the carpet in the living room, when usually the carpet is covered with a sheet of plastic. All of the families with whom I break the fast during Ramadan have enormous dining tables in formal dining rooms, but we are always on the floor and usually in the kitchen. Sitting on the floor to eat is the norm throughout much of the Middle East, and so this is not at all unusual. However, it is unusual to have the whole family together for the evening meal, because normally children have activities and husbands may be eating in the *majlis* with friends.

In Abu Dhabi, *futoor*, the Ramadan dinner, always includes *al harees*, which is heavy and almost dumpling-like, made of wheat and meat, goat or chicken usually, and takes a long time to prepare. First the ground wheat is boiled with salt and then chunks of meat are added and the mixture is left to cook for hours. When the meat has dissolved into the wheat, the pot is ready to be transferred to a hole in the ground (or into a bigger pot) and covered with hot charcoal where it is left to bubble for several more hours. After stirring with a long wooden paddle called a *midrib*, the *harees* is ready to eat. Some families serve *harees* with a drizzle of ghee, while others prefer it with an oily gravy-like rendering made from slow-cooking the remainder of the meat.

Harees, I have discovered, is the subject of much debate—rather like pumpkin pie in America: you don't like the way anyone else makes it except your own family! While it is always served at weddings (though perhaps not to the foreigners) few people take more than just a small taste and then pronounce it inedible. I have eaten more of one family's version than any other, partially due to their generosity during Ramadan when a daily pot of *harees* is delivered to my apartment door, so I too have now become a total *harees* snob.

Rice is a staple menu item, and during Ramadan there are truly mountains of rice, usually with meat of some sort or as *biryani*, a mixture that has its origins elsewhere but which is considered 'traditional' by most Emiratis, both because it is a favorite and by virtue of its long-standing place on the menu. *Biryani* originated supposedly in the Persian town of Biran, and was also a favorite in Mughal India; it is now popular as far away as Singapore, where it is called *nasi biryani*. The recipe and the ingredients for *biryani* were most probably brought to the UAE in the past by Indian and Persian traders. The meat used can be lamb, mutton, chicken or fish. *Biryani* is rich with spices, garlic and onion, fresh lemon juice, nuts and rice.

Ramadan overflows with food and cooking, and a great portion of that food leaves the kitchen in which it is prepared to be transported around the neighborhood, across the city and to mosques where men, usually migrant workers, gather to accept the generously donated food. Indeed, as much as Ramadan is about food, it is about giving—to family, to friends and to the poor. Food received at one house automatically means that another special food, perhaps a family favorite or a rare delicacy, will be in the pot or dish when it is returned. Thermal pots with lids and handles are in short supply in every house I know and most of my friends buy new as a part of Ramadan preparations. No one wants to send food to friends in a less than perfect container.

Ramadan concludes with several days of celebratory feasting, called Eid al Fitr. This is a time to visit the more far-flung family members and to call on friends. For children it means new outfits of clothes and, if they are well-behaved and lucky, it means sweets and gifts of money. During Eid my friends seem to enjoy a great sense of accomplishment and contentment—Ramadan is fulfilled. Later in the year, Eid al Adha marks the sacrifice of Abraham and is, of course, celebrated with great amounts of meat. Those families who have farms slaughter their own livestock for the feast days and often send packets of meat ready for cooking to their friends.

Sharing food is common throughout the rest of the year as well. 'If we are eating well, this is a blessing that we must share with others,' say most of the older women I know. 'It is sad, though, that what is now sent has been prepared by cooks and maids since none of our daughters know how to cook at all!' Hind exaggerates a little—some daughters do know how to cook and do it very well. Granddaughters, though, are another story altogether; most of my students have never had to boil water. In classes I ask what will happen to traditional Emirati foods if no one knows how to prepare them. Thoughtful silence follows. 'We will always have cooks who will know' is a common response. But when I point out that soon the cooks will be learning from other cooks and so it is hardly traditional, I am told that it is no different than having the date palms tended by Pakistanis or the camels cared for by Afghanis. They are correct, but that attitude is worrisome to their grandmothers. It is worrying to some of the young women too, who sometimes refer to themselves as disengaged. When I press them to explain what they mean by this, the answer is 'We have people to do everything nowadays, so what is there for us to do?'

'I am glad I am old now, old enough that I am sure that I won't have to watch our ways change more than they have already.' As she speaks, Um Abdullah is weaving stripped palm leaves. She is making a large cone-shaped basket that will be placed over food to protect it from sand and flies. 'None of my daughters or granddaughters can do this; they never wanted to learn because it takes time and patience. Of course, they don't need these basket covers any more, now that they live in big houses with fancy kitchens.' I remember my parents trying to teach me how to make jams and how to preserve foods by canning; I now wish I had learned. I confess this to Um Abdullah and we discuss the changes that come with each generation. 'Yes, I know, for our generation there wasn't much change; in fact, probably not much for my grandparents and those before either. Change might have meant that we got more fruit from Oman, and that is a small thing when I remember it now.' Her basket is giving her trouble and she yanks and stretches the edges out smoothly. 'This is not a changed life; it is a new life now. I don't mind that but it saddens me that our children have no understanding of how we did things; how we made the things we needed; how we boiled dates down to preserve them for the coming year; how we sat for hours to weave goat hair into cloth. Those things let us live, they let us live to have the children who now don't want to remember.'

Um Abdullah's sadness lifts a bit when I tell her that we have a course devoted to Emirati heritage and traditional knowledge. She agrees to come to class and teach the students how to weave. 'They won't like it,' she smiles. 'This is hard on the hands!' She shows me her calloused finger tips and dozens of tiny scars. 'But it will be good for them!'

The course on Emirati heritage is a wonderful journey of exploration into how my students and their families define and value the traditions and heritage of the past. It is common for the semester to begin with most of the students convinced that their parents know precious little about traditions such as poetry, dance and weaving. I send them home with instructions to ask questions and they report back excitedly that they have discovered that their parents are fountains of information on topics. They are incredulous to find out that their father has an enormous collection of books on poetry. They never knew he liked Nabati poetry! Their mother knows all the wonderfully scary stories about Um Al Duwais, the crone who transforms into an alluring temptress, and Bu Darya, the *jinn* who would attack ships at night. Whoever knew?

I am not sure who enjoys the class more from that point on—students or their parents! Treasure troves of material appear in class. Collections of old photos that have been hidden away in boxes are digitized and used in projects. Books, old and rather mouldy from Abu Dhabi's humidity, are lovingly restored and used in displays. Traditional technologies are almost as popular as poetry, and students investigate how healing herbs were used alongside treatments like cupping and cauterization. Children's dolls are fashioned from palm leaves and dressed with scraps of *jalabba* fabric as they were in the days before toy stores.

An integral part of this course, as well as the history course, are fieldtrips to museums, archaeological sites and historic buildings, like the fort at Faleyah in Ras al Khaimah where the first treaty was signed with the British in 1820. These bus trips have become more than a little famous for all the fun we have, but also because for many of my Abu Dhabi born students such trips are the first time they have traveled to Ras al Khaimah, and for all of them the first time they have visited historically significant sites throughout the country. Usually only one or two students have visited the National Museum in Al Ain as schoolchildren, but they've not been taken to see the Bronze Age tombs at Hili, al Jahili fort (one of the seats of power for the ruling family), the al Nahayan in Al Ain, or even the *aflaj*, the ingenious irrigation system that provided mountain water to the oases of the area.

Sadly, school curricula don't often include visiting historical sites or places of interest. The private schools, licensed to offer American, British, German, Indian and other nations' mandatory courses of study, teach very little about the UAE at all. Courses on Islam are required for Muslim students, but the history of the country is not. A significant number of Emirati students attend these private schools, as parents are keen for their children to master English at an early age. This isn't possible in the public schools because there have been few, if any, native English-speaking teachers in the classrooms, and in any event a single English language class per term is insufficient. Many parents complain that their children learn only enough to pick up the distinctive accents of their primarily Egyptian and sometimes Jordanian and Syrian teachers. Children whose mothers are not Emirati often attend private schools, as do the children of the wealthy and ruling families. The public education system has a less than stellar reputation, and parents who can afford the hefty private school tuition fees do so. Expatriate professionals are given an education or tuition subsidy for their children to attend private schools, in recognition of the fact that foreign children will return to their country of origin for further education and so must follow an American, German, French or Indian curriculum. There is too the fact that most expatriate children do not speak Arabic and so could not easily attend public school.

Quality of instruction, curriculum, facilities and classroom environments are the most common complaints about the public system. Foreign Arabs, primarily Egyptians and Jordanians along with

Sudanese, have constituted the majority of K-12 teachers from the start of public education in the country. *Freej*, the popular animated Ramadan television program, devoted an entire episode to the state of public education. The four elderly women visit the classes of one of their grandsons for parents' evening and are horrified by what they find. The Arabic language teacher is an Iranian whose pronunciation of Arabic words is so mangled that the old ladies cannot understand him; the geography teacher is a white-haired Sudanese gentleman who is convinced that the USSR still exists because it is printed on his antiquated globe; and of course the English language teacher is an Egyptian woman whose 'eeejibtshan ingaleeesh' prompted laughs and a chorus of '*bizubt*' (perfect) from the Emirati women who watched the show with me. 'That's it! It's just like that! Look, the old guy has a globe—who uses a globe now with Google Earth?' All of the women had gone to public schools themselves and all now were sending their children to private schools.

Many Emirati families, indeed the majority, don't have the option of private schools for their children because tuition is expensive, and since they receive no tuition subsidy it must be paid out of pocket. Dissatisfaction and complaints have resulted in a major overhaul of the system and many new initiatives are underway, but change will take time. I can only judge from the standard of the students entering my university classes, and this has improved tremendously in the last few years. What has not improved, and probably won't until more Emiratis are teaching in the public system, is the fact that the history and heritage of the area are sadly ignored. Actually, ignored is not the right word; de-valued is probably closer to the truth, because teachers from other Arabic-speaking countries tend to dismiss Emirati culture as 'simply Bedouin' and imply that if it were not for oil there would be nothing of value here. I know why Um Abdullah worries about her grandchildren; but my experience with students makes me more optimistic that younger Emiratis will learn about their cultural traditions and preserve many for future generations. Some traditions may not survive, and those that were developed to cope with poverty need not to survive but should be remembered.

Postscript

The global economic meltdown that began in 2007 hit Dubai hard in 2009. As much as Dubai liked to play the media darling with its plans for the biggest and the most innovative projects, perhaps it should not have been a surprise that overnight Dubai, Inc. was vilified. Dubai now was recklessly over-extended, perhaps corrupt and most certainly collapsing. The construction cranes that had dominated the city skyline for years stopped swinging around, work stopped on some projects entirely and new plans were shelved. There were stories about the numbers of people fleeing debts and abandoning cars at the airport on their way out of the country. Up the coast in Abu Dhabi life went on pretty much as usual. Banks tightened up on loans. There were rumors that the sovereign fund, Abu Dhabi Investment Authority, had taken quite a hit when Lehman Brothers collapsed, and perhaps even more when Madoff's racket was exposed, but these alleged losses in the millions did not seem to faze anyone. Yas Island, the Formula 1 race-track complex, was completed on time for the last race of the 2009 season. Construction continued apace on Saadiyat and Reem Islands, and the Raha Beach Development spread farther down the coast. Abu Dhabi was thriving; but in Abu Dhabi great concern was expressed for Dubai and what would happen there. 'Will we help them out of this?' was heard frequently. 'We cannot let Dubai sink; it will hurt the whole country! We must help them, but how much?' There were a few people who expressed something akin to *Schadenfreude*. 'Well, Dubai deserves it; they have been so caught up in being the super city of the world that they lost touch with reality.' In the end Abu Dhabi has extended a financial hand to Dubai, and when that happened even those Emiratis who had enjoyed a little of Dubai's discomfort were relieved. On the evening of the official opening of the world's tallest building, there were few in Abu Dhabi who thought that naming it Burj Khalifa was anything more than an enormous 'thank you' from Dubai.

REFERENCES

Abdullah, Muhammad Morsy, 1978. *United Arab Emirates. A Modern History.* London: Croom Helm.

Abu Lughod, Janet, 1983. 'Urbanization and Social Change in the Arab World.' *Ekistics* 50(300):223–32.

Abu Lughod, Lila, 1986. *Veiled Sentiments.* Berkeley: University of California Press.

Al Awadhi, Najla, 2007. 'Divorce and its impact on the UAE society.' In *Gulfnews.* Dubai: Al Nisr Publishing.

Al Fahim, Mohammad, 1995. *From Rags to Riches. A Story of Abu Dhabi.* London: London Centre of Arab Studies.

Al Gurg, Easa Saleh, 1998. *The Wells of Memory.* London: John Murray.

Al Qasimi, Sultan, 1986. *The Myth of Arab Piracy.* London: Croom Helm.

Al Rumaithi, H., 2008. 'A Vain Hunt for Water.' *The National.* Abu Dhabi: National Media Company.

Alsayyad, Nezar, ed., 2001. *Consuming Tradition, Manufacturing Heritage.* London: Routledge.

Anderson, B., 1983. *Imagined Communities.* London: Verso.

———, 2000. *Doing the Dirty Work. The Global Politics of Domestic Labor.* London: Zed Books.

Billig, M., 1995. *Banal Nationalism.* London: Sage.

Bristol-Rhys, Jane, 1987. 'An Ethnography of Economic Strategies Among the Urban Poor of Cairo.' Dissertation, University of Washington.

———, 2007. 'Weddings, Marriage and Money in the United Arab Emirates.' *Anthropology of the Middle East* 2(1):21–37.

———, 2009. 'Emirati Historical Narratives.' *History and Anthropology* 20(2):107–21.

Burchardt, Hermann, 2009. *Along the Gulf.* Abu Dhabi: Schiller.

Burnett, A. (ed.), 2006. *Slave Trade into Arabia.* London: Archive Editions.

Caesar, Judith, 2002. *Writing off the Beaten Track.* Syracuse: Syracuse University Press.

Codrai, Ronald, 1998a. *Dubai: a Collection of Mid-twentieth Century Photographs.* Dubai: Motivate Publishing.

REFERENCES

———, 1998b. *One Second in the Arab World: Fifty Years of Photographic Memoirs*. Dubai: Motivate Publishing.

———, 2001. *The Emirates of Yesteryear: Life in the Trucial States before the Federation of the United Arab Emirates*. London: Stacey International Publishers.

Coleman, Simon, and Mike Crang (eds.), 2002. *Tourism: Between Place and Performance*. Oxford: Berghahn Books.

Crouch, David, and Nina Lubbren (eds.), 2003. *Visual Culture and Tourism*. Oxford: Berghahn Books.

Davidson, Christopher, 2007. 'The Emirates of Abu Dhabi and Dubai: Contrasting Roles in the International System.' *Asian Affairs* 37(1):33–48.

———, 2008. *Dubai*. London: Hurst and Co.

Davies, Charles E., 1997. *The Blood Red Flag. An Investigation into Qasimi Piracy 1797–1820*. Exeter: Exeter University Press.

Dresch, Paul, 1989. *Tribes, Government and History in Yemen*. Oxford: Clarendon Press.

———, 2006. 'Foreign Matter: The Place of Strangers in Gulf Society.' In *Globalization and the Gulf*. J.W. Fox, N. Mourtada-Sabbah, and M. Al Mutawa (eds.), London: Routledge; 200–22.

Dyck, Gertrude, 1999. *The Oasis*. Dubai: Motivate Publishing.

El Guindi, Fadwa, 1999. *Veil*. New York: Berg.

El Shammaa, D., 2009. 'Uphold national identity, delegates say.' *Gulf News*. Dubai: Al Nisr.

Eriksen, T. H., 2002. *Ethnicity and Nationalism*. London: Pluto Press.

Gardner, Frank, 2003. 'Memories of a Veteran Explorer.' In *BBC World*. London.

Habboush, M., 2009. 'FNC Urges Action on Identity.' *The National*. Abu Dhabi: NMC.

Hawker, Ronald, 2008. *Building on Desert Tides*. Southampton: WIT Press.

Hawley, Donald, 1970. *The Trucial States*. London: Allen and Unwin.

Heard-Bey, Frauke, 1982. *From Trucial States to United Arab Emirates*. London: Longman.

Henderson, Edward, 1988. *This Strange Eventful History: Memoirs of Earlier Days in the UAE and Oman*. London: Quartet Books.

———, 1999. *Arabian Destiny*. Dubai: Motivate Publishing.

Hillyard, Susan, 2002. *Before the Oil: A Personal Memoir of Abu Dhabi 1954–1958*. Bakewell: Ashridge Press.

Holton, Patricia, 1991. *Mother Without a Mask*. Dubai: Motivate Publishing.

Human Rights Watch, 2009. 'UAE: Media Law Undermines Free Expression.' Human Rights Watch.

Issa, W., 2009. 'Expert sees threat to nation's existence.' *Gulf News*. Dubai: Al Nisr.

Jacob, Harold F., 2007. *Perfumes of Araby*. Reading: Garnet Publishing.

Kazim, Aqil, 2000. *The United Arab Emirates A.D. 600 to the Present*. Dubai: Gulf Book Centre.

REFERENCES

Khalaf, Sulayman, 2002. 'Globalization and Heritage Revival in the Gulf: An Anthropological Look at Dubai Heritage Village.' *Journal of Social Affairs* 19(75):13–42.

——, 2006. 'The evolution of the Gulf city type, oil and globalization.' In *Globalization and the Gulf*. J.W. Fox, N. Mourtada-Sabbah, and M. al Mutawa (eds.). London: Routledge.

Khaldun, Ibn, 1958. *The Muqaddimah. An Introduction to History*. 3 vols. (F. Rosenthal, transl.) New York: Pantheon.

Krieger, Zvika, 2007. 'Buying Culture.' In *Newsweek*, Vol. CL: 20–25.

Lane, Edward W., 1890. *An Account of the Manners and Customs of Modern Egyptians*. London: Ward, Lock and Co.

Lienhardt, P., 2001. *Shaikhdoms of Eastern Arabia*. London: Palgrave.

Meneley, Anne, 1996. *Tournaments of Value: Sociability and Hierarchy in a Yemeni Town*. Toronto: University of Toronto Press.

Nelson, Cynthia, 1973. 'Public and Private Politics:Women in the Middle Eastern World.' *American Ethnologist*: 551–63.

Onley, J., 2004. 'Britain's Native Agents in Arabia and Persia in the Nineteenth Century.' *Comparative Studies in South Asia, Africa and the Middle East* 24(1): 131–9.

——, 2005. 'Britain's Informal Empire in the Gulf, 1820–1971.' *Journal of Social Affairs* 22(87): 29–45.

Rashid, Noor Ali, 1997a. *Dubai: Life and Times* (Royal Collection). Dubai: Motivate Publishing.

——, 1997b. *The UAE: Visions of Change* (Royal Collection). Dubai: Motivate Publishing.

——, 1998. *Abu Dhabi: Life and Times*. Dubai: Motivate Publishing.

Rojek, Chris, and John Urry (eds.), 1997. *Touring Cultures*. Oxon: Routledge.

Said, Edward, 1979. *Orientalism*. New York: Vintage.

Shaw, Gareth, and Allan M. Williams (eds.), 2004. *Tourism and Tourism Spaces*. Thousand Oaks, CA: Sage.

Smith, Laurajane, 2006. *Uses of Heritage*. Oxon: Routledge.

Soffan, Linda Usra, 1980. *The Women of the United Arab Emirates*. London: Croom Helm.

Thesiger, Wilfred, 1959. *Arabian Sands*. London: Longman.

——, 1983. *The Marsh Arabs*. London: Penguin.

——, 1998. *Danakil Diary*. New York: Flamingo.

Tuson, Penelope, 2003 *Playing the Game: Western Women in Arabia*. London: I.B. Tauris.

——, 1990. (ed.) *Records of the Emirates*. Oxford: Archive Editions.

UAE, 2009. *Yearbook*. Abu Dhabi: National Media Council.

Urry, John, 2002. *The Tourist Gaze*. London: Sage.

Wehr, Hans, 1994. *Arabic English Dictionary*. J.M. Cowen (ed.). Ithaca: Spoken Language Services, Inc.

Wikan, U., 1982. *Behind the Veil in Arabia: Women in Oman*. Chicago: University of Chicago Press.

REFERENCES

Willington, Lauren, 2007. 'Abu Dhabi Thinks Ahead.' In *Construction*, Vol. 2009. Dubai: ArabianBusiness.com.

Zwemer, Samuel, 1902. 'Three Journeys in Northern Oman.' *Geographical Journal* 19.

——, 1988. *Neglected Arabia*. 8 vols. London: Archive Editions.

NOTES

1. GENERATIONS OF CHANGE

1. Kuwaiti development aid benefited the Trucial States in the years before oil, but the reports of Kuwaiti men lazing about in plush hotels in London, Cairo and Miami while Arabs from other countries fought back the Iraqis created ill-feeling that remains today.
2. Since it is considered very bad manners to inquire about a man's family, it is rare that such personal information is divulged. An exception to this was with a group of men taking an executive short course in the history of the UAE before they assumed diplomatic duties; four of the nine men had more than one wife and one of those had four wives. On the other hand, some families pride themselves on the fact that they are known for not taking more than one wife.
3. The proximity of historic Persia, the Indus Valley, Mesopotamia and Africa and the cross-Gulf trade resulted in a number of 'foreigners' in the area for hundreds of years. These people were engaged in business—mostly trade.
4. The classification of foreign workers is complex and closely monitored by the government. *Kafeel* (sponsorship) has become somewhat contentious because it appears that there is a very lucrative trade in sponsorship papers. This has been brought to light by the numbers of women sponsored by Emiratis as maids who are in fact working illegally as part-time cleaners for other people. These women pay their sponsor a fee plus all the visa costs. For a more complete discussion of foreigners see: Dresch, Paul 2006 'Foreign Matter: The Place of Strangers in Gulf Society.' In *Globalization and the Gulf.* J.W. Fox, N. Mourtada-Sabbah, and M. Al Mutawa (eds.), London: Routledge; 200–22.
5. The subtle yet rigid distinctions that divide the foreign population are the focus of my current research and will be published shortly.

6. Housing is included in most employment contracts in the UAE. In the case of Zayed University, apartments are provided as well as a cash allowance with which to purchase furniture and accessories.
7. My father headed the Division of Public Service at the American University in Cairo from 1969 to 1980 and as such consulted across the Middle East and North Africa on training programs for management and administration.
8. Some of these titles are listed in the References.

2. REPRESENTATIONS OF EMIRATIS

1. The sensation of having fallen down an Orientalist rabbit hole continued as I explored the city. The Cultural Foundation, the center for artistic and cultural events and exhibitions, proudly displays a series of paintings of Middle Eastern 'scenes' that are distinctly Orientalist in image and perspective. So too do hotels throughout the city, and I was to discover that Emiratis hang similar paintings in their homes. The larger issue of Western perceptions of Arabs, especially Arab women, and how that has shaped some of the representations made of Emiratis, is germane, of course, but far too complex and theoretically weighty to include here.
3. It was not until 1928 that a British political agent actually took up residence in Sharjah. Up until that date, officers and agents resided in Bushire, Persia or Bahrain in 1904 or on navy vessels and came ashore rarely.
4. Saadiyat, along with all major developments, are government initiatives and consequently it is often difficult to gauge people's reaction because to be critical would imply criticism of decision-makers. The complex relationship that links the ruling family to development projects is outside of my scope here but it needs to be noted that when referring to 'developments' and 'tourism' and 'hotels' in the UAE one is, by extension, also referring to a member or members of the ruling family.

3. DAYS OF THE PAST

1. It was not until the 1930s that Britain installed a British citizen in Sharjah and opened the office of the Political Resident. Prior to that, non-native agents were supervised from Bushire in Persia and later from Bahrain. In 1946 the British Bank of the Middle East opened its doors in Dubai and al Maktoum hospital was jointly funded by the ruler of

Dubai and the British. Efforts to open schools were supported primarily by Kuwait, Qatar and Egypt. The Kuwaitis very generously donated development money to the rulers of the Trucial States for schools and hospitals. For more detailed information on the complexity of the relationship between Britain and the rulers of the Trucial States, see Abdullah (1978) and Heard-Bey (1982).

2. When discussing religious views and beliefs in English my Emirati friends tend to use Allah and God interchangeably. Arabic discussions use Allah only.

4. OUR NEW LIVES BEHIND WALLS

1. In the late spring of 2007, the visa requirements for maids traveling to the UK were tightened up. I happened to be visiting a family when the mother and daughter were filling in the visa application. The maid was illiterate so she couldn't fill out the form. Required information included the maid's (employee's) monthly salary, length of time employed, language spoken, residence in the UK and, shockingly for the Emirati family, the maid was required to present herself at the British Embassy before a visa would be issued. I suggested that perhaps everyone applying for a visa must be seen in order to prevent cases of false identity. 'But she works for us and we have a house there!' In the end, the maid went to the Embassy and got her visa.

5. MARRIAGE, EDUCATION AND CHOICES

1. Engagement is the official 'writing in the book' ceremony at which the bride assents to marriage: the contract has been written and agreed upon by both families, the bride and the groom. At this point the couple are legally married and commonly refer to each other as 'husband' and 'wife,' but the marriage is not consummated until the wedding celebration occurs, and that can be weeks, months, or sometimes a year—especially if one or both of the couple are finishing their studies either in the UAE or abroad.

2. Legally dependency requires that a woman obtain the signature of her father or guardian for all official and legally binding documents and contracts. Even though entrepreneurship is encouraged for Emirati women and there are no religious prohibitions attached to women in business, the case remains that a woman has to have male validation.

3. A woman should marry a Muslim man according to religious laws, Sura II: 221, whereas a Muslim man may marry a woman who is 'ahl

141

al kitab', meaning a follower of the three revealed religions: Islam, Christianity and Judaism.

4. Alcohol is served only in bars and clubs that are connected to hotels. The connection might be somewhat tenuous, like the set-up at the Abu Dhabi Marina where there is not a hotel in sight. Many older hotels have a maze of back stairways that lead to bars hidden on mezzanines and floors that are not indicated in the elevators. These small bars are often ethnically themed—South Indian music, staff and clients in one place, Filipino in the next. The African Bar, famous for its hideously bad 'Motown' review is alas no more. I happen to live next to one hotel that has sprouted—at last count—five bars, all ethnically identified and all with discrete entries up stairs that are situated at the back of the hotel.

5. This new website is sponsored by the Ministry of Presidential Affairs. www.ihtimam.ae.

INDEX

Abu Dhabi, 3, 6, 19–23, 26, 30, 34, 40, 44, 46–7, 64–5, 74, 78, 81, 91, 94, 122; airport of, 17, 115; and Ramadan, 128; artificial islands of, 115–16, 134; Authority for Culture and Heritage, 34; economy of, 49; Emirates Palace Hotel, 37, 93; foreign influence in, 15–16; Investment Authority, 134; Mall of the Emirates, 92; National Exhibition Center, 77–9, 81; oil industry of, 5, 50; population of, 132; Qasr al Hosn, 44, 48, 50; royal families of, 120; standard of living, 57–8, 103; wealth of, 23; Zayed University, 4, 6, 15, 17, 21

Al Ain, 23, 34, 48, 58–60, 69; atmosphere of, 64; governor of, 50; National Museum, 38, 59; ruler of, 121

Arabian Peninsula: archaeological discoveries in, 119; Empty Quarter of, 98

Bedouin, 7, 28, 30, 32–4, 69; 'asabiyaa, 70; tourist relations, 36; traditions of, 20, 32, 35, 96, 117, 121

British Petroleum (BP): history of, 26

Cairo, 17, 68; American University of, 18–19

Canada: population of, 107

Christianity, 53

Dubai, 34; foreign influence in, 15

East India Company, 45

Egypt, 17, 19; population of, 18, 99, 107; Shem al Nessim celebrations, 47

Etisalat, 9

Federal National Council: representatives of, 83–4

Freej: summary of, 3–4

Gehry, Frank, 37; designer of Guggenheim, 8

Great Depression (1929): effects of, 43, 49

Hadid, Zaha: designs of, 37

Hussa, Sheikha: produce of, 60

Islam, 38, 55; and women, 52; Eid, 74, 127, 129; Jahiliyya, 119; Quran, 52, 75, 88, 127;

143

Ramadan, 12, 14, 32, 74, 127–9; *zakat*, 54

Japan: pearl industry of, 43

London, 9, 19–20, 39, 121, 125; Harrods, 8

Maktoum, Sheikh Mohammad bin Rashid al, 83

Mubarak, Sheikha Fatima bint, 80; Association for Local Women, 81

Muhammad, Prophet, 52, 119, 128; companions of, 120; Hadith of, 88

Nahayan, Sheikh Zayed Bin Sultan al: expansion of infrastructure, 50–1

Nahyan, Sheikh Khalifa bin Zayed al: Crown Prince of Abu Dhabi, 110

New York, 20

Oman: missionary presence in, 31; population of, 27, 30, 34, 100, 102, 108; traditions of, 125

Palestine, 55; population of, 100, 107

Qasimi, Sheikha Lubna al: Minister of Foreign Trade, 83

Ras al Khaimah: foreign influence in, 15

Said, Edward: *Orientalism* (1978), 68

Saadiyat Island, 37, 51, 134; Guggenheim, 8, 21, 25

Shahamma, 23

Shakhbut, Sheikh: distrust of British, 46; eccentric behaviour of,

48–9; interest in new sources of water, 48

Sharjah, 34, 67; foreign influence in, 15

Strait of Hormuz, 71

United Arab Emirates (UAE), 30, 89, 91, 97; citizenship of, 107; climate of, 1, 126, 131; charities of, 55–6; divorce rate of, 83; expatriate community of, 14, 28, 35, 125, 127–8, 132; foreign labour presence in, 15–16, 73; formation of (1971), 20; government of, 105; Higher Colleges of Technology, 11; National Day, 106; oasis economy, 60; oil industry of, 4–5, 31; population of, 7–13, 18, 25, 32, 41; standards of living, 62–4; tourist industry of, 20–1; welfare system of, 7–8

United Kingdom (UK): Foreign Service of, 31–2; naval supremacy of, 30; policies of, 50; population of, 110; presence of, 19, 28–31, 33, 45–6; treaties signed with, 131–2

United States of America (USA), 108; culinary dishes of, 128; designer fashion labels of, 76–7; population of, 110, 118

Wathba, 23

Women, 20–1, 38–40, 44, 52, 60, 74, 100; and Islam, 52; and oil industry, 47, 53; divorce of, 88; employment of, 4, 74, 83–4, 108; expatriate, 14, 19, 45, 62, 67, 113; family roles of, 12–14, 18, 21–2, 61, 69, 82–3, 87, 95–6, 98–9; fashion, 10, 33–4, 93, 97–8, 111, 125–7;

financial control of, 55, 89;
limited freedoms of, 58, 67,
72, 93, 123; older generations
of, 2–3, 62–3, 69, 112, 121–2,
127, 130, 133; perception of
foreign women, 89–92; political
activities of, 80, 83, 94, 106;
royal family members, 50, 102;
segregation of, 51, 85, 97, 121;
shopping habits of, 8, 11, 76–7;
social behaviour of, 11–12, 30,
33, 64–5, 71, 78, 84, 93–4, 99,
102, 112, 122; sporting activities of, 12; standard of living, 6,
89; traditions of, 22; weddings
of, 14, 73, 79–81, 84–7, 99,

102, 126; western perception
of, 68, 90; younger generations
of, 2, 69, 84, 98–102, 123,
127, 130
World War II, 26

Yemen, 27, 109; population of,
98, 100, 107; traditions of, 125

Zayed, Sheikh Mohammad bin,
119; Crown Prince of Abu Dhabi, 55, 107; heritage preservation activities of, 117; President
of UAE, 110; relationship with
oil industry, 120
Zayed the Great, Sheikh, 68